PARTY CAKES

PARTY
CAKES

ULTIMATE
EDITIONS

This edition published in 1995 by
Ultimate Editions
an imprint of Anness Publishing Limited
Boundary Row Studios
1 Boundary Row
London SE1 8HP

This edition exclusively distributed in Canada
by Book Express, an imprint of
RAINCOAST BOOKS DISTRIBUTION LIMITED,

Distributed in Australia by Reed Editions

© 1993 Anness Publishing Limited

Editorial Director: Joanna Lorenz
Project Editor: Judith Simons
Art Director: Peter Bridgewater
Designer: James Lawrence
Photographer: David Armstrong

Printed and bound in Singapore

Measurements

Three sets of equivalent measurements have been provided
in the recipes here, in the following order: Metric, Imperial
and American. The golden rule is never to mix the units of
measure within a recipe. The conversions are approximate,
but accurate enough to ensure successful results.

Contributors
Janice Murfitt
Angela Nilsen
Sarah Maxwell
Joanna Farrow
Louise Pickford

CONTENTS

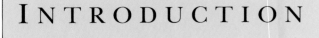

INTRODUCTION

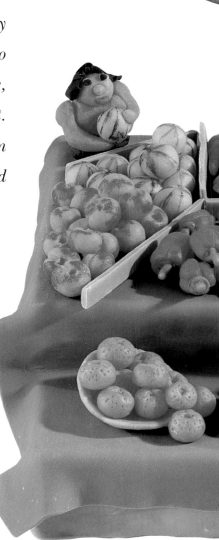

A NOVELTY CAKE *is a wonderful way to celebrate a special event or birthday, and can provide an amusing twist to traditional occasions. In the following pages, there are original cake designs for recipients of all ages, as well as unusual cakes for anniversaries and seasonal celebrations. For the kids, for instance, there are birthday balloons, a merry-go-round, or a jolly coloured snake; for adults there are cakes to suit every special interest — a mobile phone, a sailing boat, even a terracotta flower pot. There is a sophisticated egg timbale for an Easter table, and a beautiful hand-painted festive cake for Christmas.*

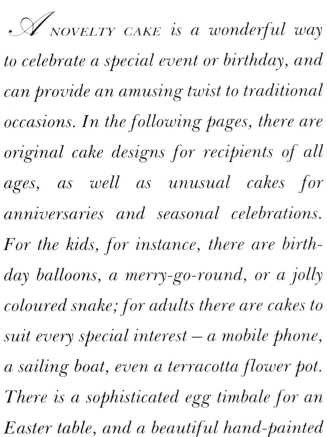

The cakes are all highly distinctive but not too difficult to achieve. There are creations using coloured sugarpaste or fondant, royal icing, butter icing, various frostings and flavoured icings. A whole range of special decorating techniques are described and explained step by step, so you can build up a whole repertoire of cake effects. A basket of strawberries is created from basketweave piping with chocolate butter icing; a candle cake shows how to marble coloured sugarpaste; a present-shaped cake uses inlaid sugarpaste in contrasting colours to spectacular effect. Follow the projects exactly or adapt the techniques to suit your own occasions.

A BASKET OF STRAWBERRIES

Quick and easy to make, a perfect surprise for a birthday or Valentine's day. And don't be put off by the icing technique – it's much easier than it looks!

INGREDIENTS

Serves 6–8
- 2-egg quantity quick-mix sponge cake
- 45 ml/3 tbsp/3 tbsp apricot glaze
- 675 g/1½ lb/1½ lb commercial or homemade marzipan
- icing (confectioners) sugar, for dusting
- 50 g/2 oz/4 tbsp caster (superfine) sugar
- 350 g/12 oz/¾ lb chocolate-flavoured butter icing
- red food colouring

MATERIALS AND EQUIPMENT

- 450 g/1 lb/3 cup loaf tin (bread pan)
- 18 cm/7 in oval cakeboard
- piping bag fitted with a small star nozzle
- 10 plastic strawberry stalks
- 30 × 7.5 cm/12 × 3 in strip kitchen foil
- 30 cm/12 in thin red ribbon

STORING

The cake can be made up to two days in advance, wrapped in foil and stored in an airtight container. The finished cake can be refrigerated for up to one week.

FREEZING

The un-iced cake can be frozen for up to three months.

VARIATION

For a Get Well cake, fill the basket with a selection of different shaped marzipan fruits. For a keen gardener, fill with marzipan vegetables.

1 Preheat the oven to 180°C/350°F/Gas 4. Grease and line the base and sides of a 450 g/1 lb/3 cup loaf tin (bread pan). Spoon the cake mixture into the prepared tin (pan) and smooth the top with a plastic spatula. Bake in the preheated oven for 40–50 minutes, or until a skewer inserted into the middle of the cake comes out clean. Leave for 5 minutes before turning out on to a wire rack to cool.

2 Slice a thin layer off the top of the cake to make it perfectly flat. Score a 5 mm/¼ in border around the edge of the cake and scrape out the insides to make a shallow hollow.

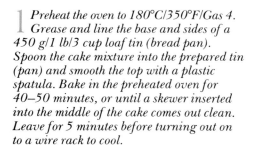

3 Place the cake in the middle of the cakeboard and brush the sides and border edges with the apricot glaze. Roll out 275 g/10 oz/10 oz of the marzipan on a surface lightly dusted with icing (confectioners) sugar. Cut the marzipan into rectangles and use to cover the sides of the cake, overlapping the border edges. Gently press the edges of the marzipan together to seal.

4 Fill the piping bag with the butter icing. Pipe vertical lines about 2.5 cm/1 in apart all around the sides of the cake. Starting at the top of the cake pipe short horizontal lines alternately crossing over and then stopping at the vertical lines to give a basket-weave effect. Pipe a decorative line of icing around the top edge of the basket, to finish.

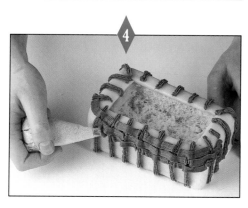

5 Colour the remaining marzipan with the red food colouring and mould into strawberry shapes. Roll in caster (superfine) sugar and press a plastic stalk into the top of each one. Carefully arrange the strawberries in the basket.

6 *To make the basket handle, fold the foil into a thin strip and wind the ribbon evenly around it to cover completely. Bend into a curve and push the ends into the sides of the cake. Decorate with ribbon bows.*

MERMAID

This mermaid cake would make a splash at any little girl's birthday party! The scales can be cut out using a 2.5 cm/1 in plain round cutter, then cut in half, if you don't have a crescent-shaped one. Use seashells, starfish or any other sea objects of your choice to decorate the sand.

INGREDIENTS

Serves 6–8

- 2-egg quantity quick-mix sponge cake
- 175 g/6 oz/6 oz butter icing
- 25 g/1 oz/1 oz plain popcorn
- 450 g/1 lb/1 lb milk chocolate, melted
- icing (confectioners) sugar, for dusting
- 225 g/8 oz/½ lb homemade or commercial marzipan
- 225 g/8 oz/½ lb sugarpaste (fondant) icing
- pink food colouring
- 1 egg white, lightly beaten
- a little sunflower oil
- 75 g/3 oz/6 tbsp demerara sugar (granulated brown sugar) for the sand

MATERIALS AND EQUIPMENT

- 1.1 l/2 pt/5 cup pudding basin (bowl)
- 25 cm/10 in fluted cakeboard
- 1 × doll, similar in dimensions to a 'Barbie' or 'Sindy' doll
- 1 small crescent-shaped cutter
- small scallop shell or shell-shaped chocolate mould

STORING

The cake can be made up to two days in advance, wrapped in foil and stored in an airtight container. The finished cake can be stored for three to four days in a cool, dry place.

FREEZING

The un-iced cake can be frozen for up to three months.

VARIATION

Flavour the sponge cake and butter icing with chocolate to make this an ideal choice for chocoholic children.

1 Preheat the oven to 180°C/350°F/Gas 4. Grease and base-line a 1.1 l/2 pint/5 cup pudding basin (bowl). Spoon the cake mixture into the prepared basin (bowl) and smooth the surface with a plastic spatula. Bake in the preheated oven for 40–50 minutes, or until a skewer inserted into the middle of the cake comes out clean. Leave for 5 minutes before turning out onto a wire rack to cool.

2 Place the cake flat side down on the work surface and cut across into 3 layers of equal thickness. Spread the bottom layer with two-thirds of the butter icing. Place the second layer of sponge cake on top and spread with the remaining butter icing. Top with the remaining piece of sponge cake. Position slightly off-centre on the cakeboard and set aside.

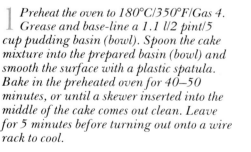

3 Mix the popcorn with about one-third of the melted chocolate and spoon around the base and up the sides of the cake. Pour the remaining melted chocolate over the top of the cake to cover completely. Leave to set at room temperature.

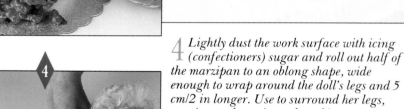

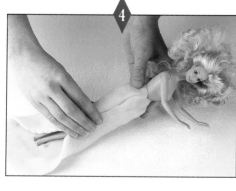

4 Lightly dust the work surface with icing (confectioners) sugar and roll out half of the marzipan to an oblong shape, wide enough to wrap around the doll's legs and 5 cm/2 in longer. Use to surround her legs, starting at the waist and working downwards. Mould the bottom section into a fin-shaped tail. Position the doll so she is sitting on the cake.

5 Divide the sugarpaste (fondant) in half; colour one half dark pink and the other half light pink with pink food colouring. Thinly roll out the dark pink sugarpaste (fondant) on a work surface lightly dusted with icing (confectioners) sugar. Reserve a small piece of the sugarpaste (fondant) to make the mermaid's top. Cut out 'scales' with a small crescent-shaped cutter, keeping the cut scales covered with a sheet of cling film (plastic wrap) to stop them drying out. Thinly roll out the light pink sugarpaste (fondant) icing and continue to cut out the scales in the same way.

6 To make the bodice, press the reserved piece of dark pink sugarpaste (fondant) icing over an oiled tiny scallop shell, or into an oiled shell-shaped chocolate mould. Gently remove the sugarpaste (fondant) from the mould and trim the edges. Brush with a little egg white and stick in place for the mermaid's top.

Brush each scale with a little egg white and, starting at the fin end, stick on to the tail in overlapping rows, until the marzipan is completely covered.

7 Sprinkle the cakeboard with demerara (granulated brown) sugar for the sand and decorate with seashells, starfish or any other sea objects of your choice.

LADYBIRD

Create a little animal magic and make this cake
for a nature lover or gardener.

INGREDIENTS

Serves 10–12

- 3-egg quantity lemon-flavoured
  quick mix sponge cake
- 175 g/6 oz/6 oz lemon-flavoured
  butter icing
- 60 ml/4 tbsp/4 tbsp lemon curd,
  warmed
- icing (confectioners) sugar, for
  dusting
- good 1 kg/2 lb 6 oz/2 lb 6 oz
  sugarpaste (fondant) icing
- red, black and green food
  colourings
- 5 marshmallows
- 50 g/2 oz/2 oz golden commercial
  or homemade marzipan
- edible ladybird icing decorations
  (optional)

MATERIALS AND EQUIPMENT

- 1.1 l/2 pt/5 cup ovenproof mixing
  bowl
- greaseproof (wax) paper
- wooden skewer
- 28 cm/11 in round cakeboard
- 4 cm/1½ in plain round biscuit
  (cookie) cutter
- 5 cm/2 in plain round biscuit
  (cookie) cutter
- garlic press
- 2 pipe cleaners

STORING

The cake can be made up to two
days in advance, wrapped in foil and
stored in an airtight container. The
finished cake, covered in sugarpaste
(fondant), can be stored for three to
four days in a cool, dry place.

FREEZING

The un-iced cake can be frozen for
up to three months.

VARIATION

Marzipan works just as well as a
covering for this cake.

1 Preheat the oven to 180°C/350°F/Gas 4.
Grease and line the base of a 1.1 l/2 pt/5
cup ovenproof mixing bowl. Spoon the
mixture into the prepared bowl and smooth
the surface with a plastic spatula. Bake in
the preheated oven for 55–60 minutes, or
until a skewer inserted into the centre of the
cake comes out clean. Leave for 5 minutes
before turning out on to a wire rack to cool.

2 Cut the cake across in half and sandwich
together with the butter icing. Cut
vertically through the cake, about a third of
the way in. Brush both pieces of cake with
the lemon curd.

3 Colour 450 g/1 lb/1 lb sugarpaste
(fondant) icing red, with red food
colouring. Lightly dust the work surface
with icing (confectioners) sugar and roll out
the red sugarpaste (fondant) to about 5
mm/¼ in thick. Use to cover the larger piece
of cake to make the ladybird's body. Use a
wooden skewer or the back of a knife to
make an indentation down the centre of the
cake for the wings.

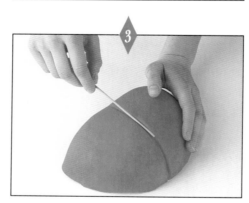

4 Colour 350 g/12 oz/¾ lb sugarpaste
(fondant) icing black, with black food
colouring. Roll out three-quarters of the
black sugarpaste (fondant) and use to cover
the smaller piece of cake for the ladybird's
head. Place the cakes on the cakeboard,
assembling the ladybird and lightly pressing
the head and body together to shape.

5 Roll out 50 g/2 oz/2 oz sugarpaste
(fondant) icing and cut out two circles
with a 5 cm/2 in round biscuit (cookie)
cutter for the eyes. Brush with a little water
and stick in position on the head.

6 Roll out the remaining black sugarpaste
(fondant) icing thinly. Use to cut out
eight circles with a 4 cm/1½ in round
biscuit (cookie) cutter. Use two of these
rounds for the eyes and stick the others on to
the body with a little water. Reserve the
trimmings.

7 Colour 225 g/8 oz/½ lb sugarpaste
(fondant) icing green. To make the
grass, break off pieces of green sugarpaste
(fondant) and squeeze through a garlic
press. Trim off with a knife. Brush the
board around the ladybird with a little
water and gently stick down the grass.

8 To make the marshmallow flowers, roll the marzipan into a 2 cm/³/4 in long sausage shape and cut into slices to make rounds. Set aside. Dust the work surface with a little icing (confectioners) sugar and flatten each marshmallow with a rolling pin, sprinkling with more icing (confectioners) sugar to prevent sticking. Using scissors, snip from the outside edge towards the middle of each marshmallow to make the petals. Press a marzipan round into the middle of each flower and use to decorate the cake.

9 To make the antennae, paint the pipe cleaners with black food colouring and press a small ball of the remaining black sugarpaste (fondant) on to the end of each one. Bend each pipe cleaner slightly and insert it into the cake between the head and the body. Arrange the decorations around the cake, if using.

PIZZA CAKE

Quick, easy and impressive – a definite winner
for pizza fanatics everywhere.

INGREDIENTS

Serves 8–10
- 2-egg quantity quick-mix sponge cake
- 350 g/12 oz/³/4 lb butter icing, coloured red
- 175 g/6 oz/6 oz yellow commercial or homemade marzipan
- 15 ml/1 tbsp/1 tbsp desiccated (shredded) coconut
- red and green food colouring
- icing (confectioners) sugar, for dredging
- 25 g/1 oz/1 oz sugarpaste (fondant) icing

MATERIALS AND EQUIPMENT

- 23 cm/9 in shallow cake tin (pan)
- greaseproof (wax) paper
- 25 cm/10 in pizza plate
- cheese grater
- a leaf cutter or stencil

STORING

The cake can be made up to two days in advance, wrapped in foil and stored in an airtight container. The finished cake can be refrigerated for up to one week.

FREEZING

The un-iced cake can be frozen for up to three months.

1 Preheat the oven to 180°C/350°F/Gas 4. Grease and line the base of a 23 cm/9 in shallow cake tin (pan). Spoon the mixture into the prepared tin (pan) and smooth the surface with a plastic spatula. Bake in the preheated oven for 40–50 minutes, or until a skewer inserted into the centre of the cake comes out clean. Leave for 5 minutes before turning out onto a wire rack to cool.

2 Place the cake on the pizza plate and spread evenly with the red butter icing, leaving a 1 cm/½ in border around the edge.

3 Knead the marzipan for a few minutes, to soften slightly, then grate it in the same way as grating cheese. Use to sprinkle over the red butter icing.

4 Colour the sugarpaste (fondant) icing green with green food colouring. For the leaf garnish, lightly dust the work surface with icing (confectioners) sugar and roll out the green sugarpaste (fondant) to about 5 mm/¼ in thick. Use the leaf cutter or stencil to cut out two leaf shapes. Garnish the pizza cake with the sugarpaste (fondant) leaves.

5 To make the chopped herbs, place the desiccated (shredded) coconut in a small bowl and add enough green food colouring to make it dark green, stirring after each addition of colouring.

6 Scatter the coconut herbs over the pizza cake.

THE BEAUTIFUL PRESENT CAKE

For a best friend, mother, aunt, grandmother or sister, this beautiful cake is fitting for any occasion.

INGREDIENTS

Serves 15–20
- 4-egg quantity vanilla-flavoured quick-mix sponge cake
- 350 g/12 oz/³⁄₄ lb vanilla-flavoured butter icing
- 60 ml/4 tbsp/4 tbsp apricot glaze
- icing (confectioners) sugar, for dusting
- 575 g/1¹⁄₄ lb/1¹⁄₄ lb homemade or commercial marzipan
- 850 g/1 lb 14 oz/1 lb 14 oz sugarpaste (fondant) icing
- purple and pink food colouring
- cold water, for brushing

MATERIALS AND EQUIPMENT

- 23 cm/9 in square cake tin (pan)
- 25 cm/10 in square cakeboard
- heart-shaped biscuit (cookie) cutter
- small brush
- small fluted carnation cutter
- cocktail stick
- pink food-colouring pen

STORING

The cake can be made up to two days in advance, wrapped in foil and stored in an airtight container. The finished cake, covered in sugarpaste (fondant), can be stored for three to four days in a cool, dry place.

FREEZING

The un-iced cake can be frozen for up to three months.

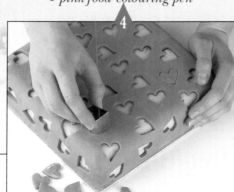

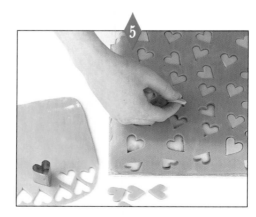

1 Preheat the oven to 180°C/350°F/Gas 4. Grease and line the base and sides of a 23 cm/9 in cake tin (pan). Spoon the mixture into the prepared tin (pan) and smooth the surface with a plastic spatula. Bake in the preheated oven for 1¹⁄₄–1¹⁄₂ hours, or until a skewer inserted into the centre of the cake comes out clean. Leave for 5 minutes before turning out onto a wire rack to cool.

2 Cut the cake in half horizontally and spread with the vanilla butter icing. Sandwich with the top sponge cake and place the cake in the centre of the cakeboard. Brush the cake with apricot glaze. Lightly dust the work surface with icing (confectioners) sugar and roll out the marzipan to about ¹⁄₂ cm/¹⁄₄ in thick. Use to cover the cake.

3 Colour 575 g/1¹⁄₄ lb/1¹⁄₄ lb sugarpaste (fondant) icing purple. Roll out the purple sugarpaste (fondant) on the work surface, lightly dusted with icing (confectioners) sugar. Use to cover the cake, smoothing down the sides gently and trimming away any excess sugarpaste (fondant).

4 Using the heart-shaped cutter, stamp out hearts all over the cake to make an even pattern. Remove the purple hearts with a small, sharp knife, taking care not to damage the surrounding sugarpaste (fondant). Knead the hearts together and keep this reserved purple sugarpaste (fondant) in a plastic bag to use later.

5 Colour 275 g/10 oz/10 oz sugarpaste (fondant) icing pink. Roll out to about ¹⁄₂ cm/¹⁄₄ in thick on a work surface, lightly dusted with icing (confectioners) sugar. Use the heart-shaped cutter to cut out as many hearts as you need to fill the spaces left by the purple ones on the cake, re-rolling the pink sugarpaste (fondant), as necessary. Reserve the excess. Carefully insert the pink hearts into the spaces.

6 Roll out the reserved pink sugarpaste (fondant) to about ¹⁄₂ cm/¹⁄₄ in thick on a work surface, lightly dusted with icing (confectioners) sugar and cut into three strips about 2 cm/³⁄₄ in wide and 30 cm/12 in long. Lay one strip across the centre of the cake and another at right angles across the centre, brushing the strips with a little water to secure. Trim away any excess sugarpaste (fondant) at the edges, if necessary. Reserve all the trimmings.

7 To make the bow, divide the remaining strip of pink sugarpaste (fondant) icing into quarters. Loop two of the quarters and seal the joins with a little water. Position at the centre of the cake, where the strips cross. Trim the ends of the remaining quarters to look like the ends of bows and overlap them across the joining of the loops; secure with a little water. Reserve the trimmings.

8 To make the flowers, roll out the remaining purple and pink sugarpaste (fondant) on a work surface, lightly dusted with icing (confectioners) sugar. Cut out two 1/2 cm/1/4 in thick fluted rounds from each colour, using the carnation cutter.

9 With a cocktail stick or toothpick, carefully roll out the edges of each fluted round to make the frilled petals. Use a little of the purple sugarpaste (fondant) to make two tiny balls for the centres of the flowers. Then, using a little water, place a pink flower on top of a purple one and the tiny ball in the centre. Carefully lift and pinch behind the flower to secure. Repeat with the other flower and position them both on the cake. Mould together any remaining sugarpaste (fondant), roll out and cut into a pretty tag. Write a name or short message using the food-colouring pen and position on the cake.

SAILING BOAT

Make this cake for someone who loves sailing or is going on a journey – you can even personalize the cake with a rice paper nametag flag, written with a food-colouring pen.

INGREDIENTS

Serves 10–12

- 3-egg quantity quick-mix sponge cake
- 60 ml/4 tbsp/4 tbsp apricot glaze
- 450 g/1 lb/1 lb sugarpaste (fondant) icing
- 1 grissini (bread stick)
- 1 sheet of rice paper
- 9 short candy sticks
- 4 Polo (Lifesaver) mints
- 1 thin red 'bootlace' liquorice strip
- 1 thin black 'bootlace' liquorice strip
- 1 black liquorice Catherine wheel, with an orange sweet in the centre
- 1 blue sherbet 'flying saucer'
- 350 g/12 oz/3/4 lb butter icing coloured blue
- blue food colouring

MATERIALS AND EQUIPMENT

- 900 g/2 lb/5 cup loaf tin (bread pan)
- greaseproof (wax) paper
- 33 × 18 cm/13 × 7 in cakeboard
- 1 cocktail stick or toothpick
- black food-colouring pen

STORING

The cake can be made up to two days in advance, wrapped in foil and stored in an airtight container. The finished cake, covered in sugarpaste (fondant), can be stored for three to four days in a cool, dry place.

FREEZING

The un-iced cake can be frozen for up to three months.

VARIATION

To make this boat even more colourful, draw an attractive design on the sails using coloured pens. Remember that only the special cake decorating pens contain edible inks, so if you use another type of pen, don't eat the sails.

1 Preheat the oven to 180°C/350°F/Gas 4. Grease and line the base and sides of a 900 g/2 lb/5 cup loaf tin (bread pan). Spoon the cake mixture into the prepared tin (pan) and smooth the top with a plastic spatula. Bake in the preheated oven for 55–60 minutes, or until a skewer inserted into the centre of the cake comes out clean. Leave for 5 minutes before turning out on to a wire rack to cool.

2 Slice a thin layer off the top of the cake to make it perfectly flat. Trim one end to make a pointed bow. Using a small sharp knife, cut a shallow hollow from the centre of the cake, leaving a 1 cm/1/2 in border.

3 Brush the cake all over with the apricot glaze. Roll out the sugarpaste (fondant) icing to 35 × 23 cm/14 × 9 in rectangle and lay over the cake. Gently ease the sugarpaste (fondant) into the hollow middle and down the sides of the cake, until completely and evenly covered. Trim the edges at the base.

4 Cover the cakeboard with the blue butter icing, peaking it to resemble a rough sea. Position the cake on the iced board. Cut the rice paper into two tall triangular sails. Using a small brush, apply a little water along the length of the grissini (bread) stick and secure the rice paper sails to it. Insert the mast into the front of the hollowed compartment at the bow of the boat, pushing through the cake to the board.

5 Insert seven of the short candy sticks around the bow of the boat, leaving a little space between each one and allowing them to stand about 2.5 cm/1 in above the surface of the cake. Insert the remaining two short candy sticks at either side of the stern of the boat and hang two Polo (Lifesaver) mints on each, for the life belts. Use the bootlace liquorice strips to tie loosely in and out of the candy sticks at the bow of the boat for the guard rail. Trim away any excess, if necessary.

6 *Cut a small flag shape from the remaining rice paper and personalize it using the food colour pen. Stick on to the cocktail stick using a little water and position the flag at the stern of the boat.*

7 *Uncoil the liquorice Catherine wheel and remove the sweet from the centre. Use the liquorice to make a fender all around the outside of the boat, securing it with a little water. Trim the excess and use the remainder to line the seating area in the same way. Position the sweet from the centre of the Catherine wheel to one side of the boat for the searchlight. Place the sherbet flying saucer in the seating area for the cushion.*

SHIRT AND TIE CAKE

Instead of buying the man in your life yet another shirt and tie for his birthday, make him a cake for a deliciously novel surprise!

INGREDIENTS

Serves 20–30

- 4-egg quantity coffee-flavoured quick-mix sponge cake
- 350 g/12 oz/¾ lb coffee-flavoured butter icing
- 90 ml/6 tbsp/6 tbsp apricot glaze
- icing (confectioners) sugar, for dusting
- good 1 kg/2 lb 6 oz/2 lb 6 oz sugarpaste (fondant) icing
- blue food colouring
- 125 g/4 oz/1 cup icing (confectioners) sugar, sifted
- 45–60 ml/3–4 tbsp/3–4 tbsp water

MATERIALS AND EQUIPMENT

- 19 × 26.5 cm/7½ × 10½ in roasting tin (pan)
- greaseproof (wax) paper
- 30 × 32.5 cm/12 × 13 in cakeboard
- steel ruler
- wooden skewer
- piping bag fitted with a small round nozzle
- 40 × 5 cm/16 × 2 in piece of flexible card, the short ends cut at an angle, for the collar
- small brush
- 'Happy Birthday' cake decoration (optional)
- blue tissue paper (optional)

STORING

The cake can be made up to two days in advance, wrapped in foil and stored in an airtight container. The finished cake, covered in sugarpaste (fondant), can be stored for three to four days in a cool, dry place.

FREEZING

The un-iced cake can be frozen for up to three months.

VARIATION

Choose your own colour contrasts for the shirt and the tie to suit the man; for example, a blue or red collar on a white or red shirt with a zany yellow tie!

1 Preheat the oven to 180°C/350°F/Gas 4. Grease and line the base and sides of a 19 × 26.5 cm/7½ × 10½ in roasting tin (pan). Spoon the mixture into the prepared tin (pan) and smooth the surface with a plastic spatula. Bake in the preheated oven for 1¼–1½ hours, or until a skewer inserted into the centre of the cake comes out clean. Leave for 5 minutes before turning out on to a wire rack to cool.

2 Cut the cake in half horizontally and spread with the coffee-flavoured butter icing. Sandwich together with the top half of the sponge cake. Brush the cake evenly with the apricot glaze and lightly dust the work surface with icing (confectioners) sugar. Colour 675 g/1½ lb/1½ lb sugarpaste (fondant) icing light blue. Roll out the light blue sugarpaste (fondant) to about 5 mm/¼ in thick and use to cover the cake, gently easing the sugarpaste (fondant) down the sides and corners. Trim away any excess icing. Place the cake on the cakeboard.

3 Using a steel ruler, make grooves down the length and sides of the cake, in straight lines, about 2.5 cm/1 in apart. Use a wooden skewer to re-indent the grooves, rolling the skewer slightly from side to side to make the channels deeper and slightly wider.

4 Mix the icing (confectioners) sugar and water together in a small bowl to make a just thick glacé icing and use to fill the piping bag fitted with the small, round nozzle. Pipe lines of glacé icing into the grooves on the top and sides of the cake, moving slowly and evenly for the best results.

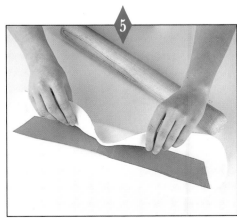

5 To make the collar, roll out 225 g/
8 oz/¹/₂ lb sugarpaste (fondant) icing,
on a work surface lightly dusted with icing
(confectioners) sugar, to a 40.5 × 10 cm/
16¹/₂ × 4 in rectangle. Lay the piece of
card for the collar on top, placing it along
one edge of the sugarpaste (fondant). Brush
a little water around the edges of the
sugarpaste (fondant), then carefully lift the
other edge of the sugarpaste (fondant) and
fold over the card to encase it completely.
Trim the two short ends to match the angles
of the card. Carefully lift the collar and
gently bend it round and position on the
cake, applying a little water to help secure it
in place.

6 Colour 175 g/6 oz/6 oz sugarpaste
(fondant) icing dark blue. To make the
tie, cut off one-third of the dark blue
sugarpaste (fondant) and shape into a
pyramid for the tie knot. Position the knot.
Lightly dust the work surface with icing
(confectioners) sugar and roll out the
remaining dark blue sugarpaste (fondant)
icing to about 5 mm/¹/₄ in thick. Cut out a
tie piece to fit under the knot and long
enough to hang over the edge of the cake,
making it slightly wider at the end where
you cut a point. Position the tie piece,
tucking it under the knot and applying a
little water to secure it in place. Finish the
cake with the 'Happy Birthday' decoration
and tissue paper, if using.

MERRY-GO-ROUND CAKE

Choose your own figures to sit on the merry-go-round, from chocolate animals to jelly bears.

Remember to position the top of the merry-go-round at the last minute for the best results.

INGREDIENTS

Serves 16–20

- 3-egg quantity lemon-flavoured quick-mix sponge cake
- 60 ml/4 tbsp/4 tbsp apricot glaze
- icing (confectioners) sugar, to dust
- 575 g/1¼ lb/1¼ lb sugarpaste (fondant) icing
- orange and yellow food colouring
- 8 × 18 cm/7 in long candy sticks
- sweet (candy) figures

MATERIALS AND EQUIPMENT

- 2 × 20 cm/8 in round sandwich cake tins (pans)
- greaseproof (wax) paper
- 23 cm/9 in round fluted cakeboard
- 18 cm/7 in round piece of stiff card
- cocktail stick or toothpick
- 2 different sizes of star-shaped biscuit (cookie) cutters

STORING

The cake can be made up to two days in advance, wrapped in foil and stored in an airtight container. The finished cake, covered in sugarpaste (fondant), can be stored for three to four days in a cool, dry place.

FREEZING

The un-iced cake can be frozen for up to three months.

1 Preheat the oven to 180°C/350°F/Gas 4. Grease and line the bases of two 20 cm/8 in round sandwich tins (pans). Spoon two-thirds of the mixture into one tin (pan) and the other third into the other tin (pan). Smooth the surfaces with a plastic spatula. Bake for 55–60 minutes, or until a skewer inserted into the centre of each cake comes out clean. Leave for 5 minutes before turning out onto a wire rack to cool.

2 Place the larger cake, upside-down, on the fluted cakeboard to make the base of the merry-go-round, and place the smaller cake, right-side up, on the piece of card. Brush both cakes evenly with the apricot glaze and set aside. Lightly dust the work surface with icing (confectioners) sugar and place 450 g/1 lb/1 lb sugarpaste (fondant) icing on it. Using the cocktail stick or toothpick, apply a few spots of the orange food colouring to the sugarpaste (fondant).

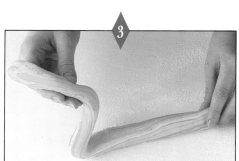

3 To achieve the marbled effect in the sugarpaste (fondant) icing, roll into a sausage shape on the work surface. Fold the sausage shape in half and continue to roll out until it reaches its original length. Fold over again and roll out again into a sausage shape. Continue this process until the fondant is streaked with the orange colour.

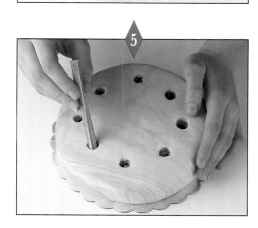

4 Divide the marbled sugarpaste (fondant) into two-thirds and one third. Roll out the larger portion on the work surface lightly dusted with icing (confectioners) sugar and use to cover the larger cake. Repeat with the smaller portion of marbled sugarpaste (fondant) and use to cover the smaller cake. Trim away any excess sugarpaste (fondant) and reserve, wrapped in cling film (plastic wrap).

5 Using one of the candy sticks, make eight holes at even distances around the edge of the larger cake, leaving about a 2 cm/¾ in border. Press the upright stick right through the cake to the board. Knead the reserved marbled sugarpaste (fondant) until the orange colour is evenly blended, then roll out on the work surface lightly dusted with icing (confectioners) sugar. Using the smaller star cutter, cut out nine stars. Cover with cling film (plastic wrap) and set aside. Colour 125 g/4 oz/¼ lb sugarpaste (fondant) icing yellow. Roll out on a surface lightly dusted with icing (confectioners) sugar and cut out nine stars with the larger star cutter. Sit the smaller cake on an upturned bowl and stick eight larger and eight smaller stars around the edge of the cake, using a little water to secure. Stick the remaining stars on top of the cake.

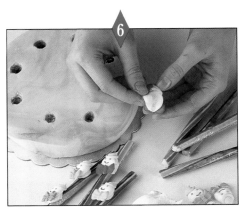

6 To secure the sweet figures to the candy sticks, stick tiny balls of the excess sugarpaste (fondant) behind the figures and then lightly press onto the sticks. Leave to set for about 30 minutes. Place the candy sticks in the holes on the larger cake.

7 To assemble the cake, carefully lift the smaller cake, with its card base, onto the candy sticks, making sure it balances before letting go!

MOBILE PHONE CAKE

For the upwardly mobile man, this novel cake is the business!

INGREDIENTS

Serves 8–10

- 2-egg quantity vanilla-flavoured quick-mix sponge cake
- 30 ml/2 tbsp/2 tbsp apricot glaze
- icing (confectioners) sugar, for dusting
- 375 g/13 oz/13 oz sugarpaste (fondant) icing
- black food colouring
- 10 small square sweets (candies)
- 1–2 stripey liquorice sweets (candies)
- 30–45 ml/2–3 tbsp/2–3 tbsp icing (confectioners) sugar
- 2.5–5 ml/½–1 tsp/½–1 tsp water

MATERIALS AND EQUIPMENT

- 900 g/2 lb/5 cup loaf tin (bread pan)
- 23 × 18 cm/9 × 7 in cakeboard
- diamond-shaped biscuit (cookie) cutter
- small brush
- small strip of kitchen foil
- piping bag fitted with a small round nozzle

STORING

The cake can be made up to two days in advance, wrapped in foil and stored in an airtight container. The finished cake, covered in sugarpaste (fondant), can be stored for three to four days in a cool, dry place.

FREEZING

The un-iced cake can be frozen for up to three months.

1 Preheat the oven to 180°C/350°F/Gas 4. Grease and line the base and sides of a 900 g/2 lb/5 cup loaf tin (bread pan). Spoon the mixture into the prepared tin (pan) and smooth the surface with a plastic spatula. Bake in the preheated oven for 40–50 minutes, or until a skewer inserted into the centre of the cake comes out clean. Leave for 5 minutes before turning out on to a wire rack to cool.

2 Turn the cake upside-down and starting about 2.5 cm/1 in along the cake, slice into it, across and at an angle, about 1 cm/½ in deep. Cut out this wedge, then slice horizontally along the length of the cake, stopping about 2.5 cm/1 in away from the end. Withdraw the knife and re-insert it at the end of the cake and slice into the cake to meet up with the horizontal cut. Remove the inner piece of cake and discard.

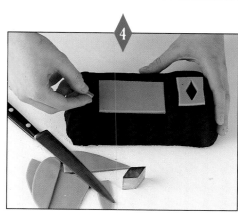

3 Place the cake on the cakeboard. Brush the cake evenly with the apricot glaze. Colour 275 g/10 oz/10 oz sugarpaste (fondant) icing black. Lightly dust the work surface with icing (confectioners) sugar and roll out the black sugarpaste (fondant) to about 5 mm/¼ in thick. Use to cover the cake, carefully smoothing the sugarpaste (fondant) into the carved shape of the cake and down the sides and corners. Trim away any excess sugarpaste (fondant) and reserve, wrapped in cling film (plastic wrap).

4 Colour 75 g/3 oz/3 oz sugarpaste (fondant) icing grey, with a little black food colouring. Roll out the grey sugarpaste (fondant) to about 5 mm/¼ in thick on a work surface lightly dusted with icing (confectioners) sugar. Cut out one piece of sugarpaste (fondant) to fit the centre of the cake, leaving a 1 cm/½ in border and another piece, about 2.5 cm/1 in square. Using the diamond-shaped biscuit (cookie) cutter, stamp out the centre of the square. Place the diamond at the bottom of the phone, and the square at the top. Position the piece of sugarpaste (fondant) for the centre, securing all the grey pieces with a small brush dipped in a little water.

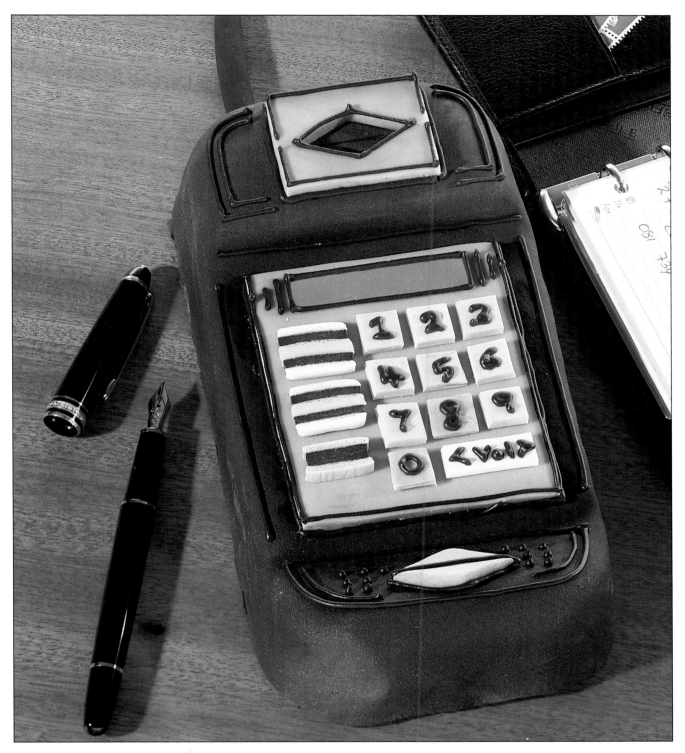

5 *Position the sweets (candies) and the strip of kitchen foil for the dial pad. To make the glacé icing, mix the icing (confectioners) sugar with the water and black food colouring, until of piping consistency. Fill the piping bag fitted with the small, round nozzle and pipe border lines around the edges of the phone, including the grey pieces of sugarpaste (fondant). Pipe the numbers on the keys.*

6 *Knead the reserved black sugarpaste (fondant) and use to roll into a sausage shape for the aerial. Indent the top with a knife and position at the top of the phone, to one side. Secure with a little water.*

RAINBOW SNAKE CAKE

This wild cake needs no cooking. It uses leftover sponge-cake crumbs – or you can buy a sponge cake and grind it yourself. Its heavy texture and sweet flavour make it an excellent party cake, for kids or adults. You only need serve a little, so it goes a long way. For a large party, double the ingredients to make an extra big snake. Use rubber gloves to protect your hands when colouring the marzipan and remember to wash them between colours.

INGREDIENTS

Serves 10–15
- 175 g/6 oz/3 cups plain sponge-cake crumbs
- 175 g/6 oz/1½ cups ground almonds
- 75 g/3 oz/6 tbsp light brown muscovado (molasses) sugar
- 5 ml/1 tsp/1 tsp ground mixed spice
- 2.5 ml/½ tsp/½ tsp ground cinnamon
- 45 ml/3 tbsp/3 tbsp fresh orange juice
- finely grated zest of 1 orange
- 75 ml/5 tbsp/5 tbsp clear runny honey or golden syrup (light corn syrup)
- 675 g/1½ lb/1½ lb white commercial or homemade marzipan
- icing (confectioners) sugar, for dusting
- red, yellow, orange, violet and green food colouring
- 2 red sugar-coated chocolate Smarties (M&Ms)
- 125 g/4 oz/2 cups desiccated (shredded) coconut
- wine-gum (chewy) snake sweets (optional)

MATERIALS AND EQUIPMENT

- 5 cocktail sticks
- rolling pin
- 25 cm/10 in round cakeboard
- small piece of thin red card cut into a tongue shape
- small star-shaped cutter
- small brush

STORING

The marzipan-iced cake can be made up to four days in advance and stored in an airtight container in a cool, dry place.

FREEZING

Not recommended.

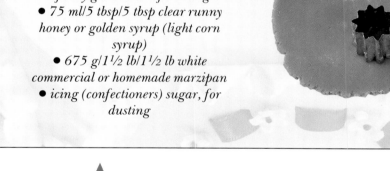

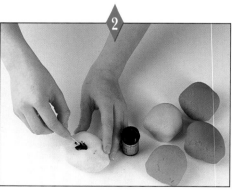

1 In a large mixing bowl, combine the cake crumbs, almonds, sugar, spices, orange juice and zest and the honey. Stir well until all the ingredients hold together in a moist, thick paste. Set aside.

2 To colour the marzipan, divide it into five equal portions. Lightly dust the work surface with icing (confectioners) sugar and apply one of the food colourings to one of the portions of marzipan, using a cocktail stick or toothpick. Knead the colour into the marzipan, until evenly blended. Clean the work surface and lightly dust again with icing (confectioners) sugar. Take another piece of marzipan and apply another of the colourings. Repeat this process, until all five portions of marzipan are different colours, using a new cocktail stick (toothpick) each time. Remove a tiny ball from the green portion and reserve, covered in cling film (plastic wrap).

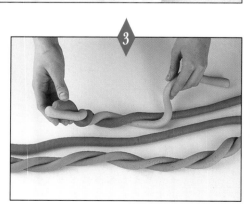

3 Using your hands, roll each piece of marzipan out on a work surface lightly dusted with icing (confectioners) sugar, to a sausage shape, about 1 cm/½ in diameter. Line up the sausage shapes next to each other on the work surface and twist together the two outside sausages, leaving only the centre sausage untouched. Push the two outside twists together to squeeze against the middle sausage firmly.

4 Use a little icing (confectioners) sugar to dust the rolling pin and make short, sharp downward movements starting at one end, rolling the marzipan out a little at a time to about 15 cm/6 in wide. Keep the rolled width even all along the snake. Carefully slide a heavy, sharp knife underneath the rolled out marzipan to unstick it from the work surface. Flip the rolled out marzipan over, taking care not to tear it.

5 Spoon the cake-crumb mixture evenly down the centre of the marzipan, using your hands to form it into a firm sausage shape. Starting at one end, gather up the sides of the marzipan around the cake mixture, pinching the sides together firmly to seal, until the cake mixture is completely encased. Shape the head by flattening the marzipan slightly, and the tail by squeezing it into a tapered end. Roll the snake over so the seal lies underneath.

6 Carefully slide the snake on to the cakeboard, tail-end first, coiling it round as you go. The head can either be propped up on an extra lump of marzipan or left to flop over the rest of the snake. Both methods look very effective. Make a small incision where the mouth would be and insert the red tongue. Roll the reserved green marzipan out on a work surface lightly dusted with icing (confectioners) sugar and cut out two eyes, using the small star cutter. Position the eyes, securing them with a small brush dipped in a little water. Press the small Smarties or M&Ms on top.

7 Place the desiccated (shredded) coconut in a bowl and add a few spots of green food colouring with a little water. Stir until the coconut is flecked green. Scatter around the snake on the board to make the grass. Decorate with the wine-gum (chewy candy) snakes, if using.

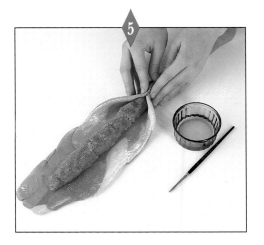

EASTER CAKE

An unusual presentation for a spicy Easter fruit cake. The cake is covered with marzipan and chocolate moulding icing, then finished with ribbons and eggs made from chocolate modelling paste. The cake can be completed up to four weeks in advance.

INGREDIENTS

Serves 16
- 125 g/4 oz/¹/2 cup softened butter or margarine
- 125 g/4 oz/¹/2 cup light brown sugar
- 3 eggs
- 175 g/6 oz/1¹/2 cups plain (all-purpose) flour
- 10 ml/2 tsp/2 tsp ground mixed spice
- 400 g/14 oz/3¹/2 cups mixed dried fruit
- 50 g/2 oz/¹/4 cup glacé cherries, chopped
- 50 g/2 oz/¹/4 cup hazelnuts
- 45 ml/3 tbsp/3 tbsp apricot glaze
- 450 g/1 lb/1 lb homemade or commercial marzipan
- brown food colouring

MATERIALS AND EQUIPMENT

- 1.5 l/2¹/2 pt/3 pt pudding basin (bowl)
- greaseproof (wax) paper
- 25 cm/10 in round gold cakeboard
- clean piece sponge
- several squares of gold foil, about 6.5 cm/2¹/2 in in diameter
- paintbrush

STORING

The iced cake can be covered loosely in foil and stored in a cool dry place for up to four weeks.

FREEZING

The fruit cake can be frozen for up to six months.

CHOCOLATE MOULDING ICING

- 100 g/4 oz/4 squares plain (semisweet) or milk chocolate
- 30 ml/2 tbsp/2 tbsp liquid glucose
- 1 egg white
- 450 g/1 lb/3¹/2 cups icing (confectioners) sugar
- cornflour (cornstarch) for dusting

CHOCOLATE MODELLING PASTE

- 50 g/2 oz/2 squares plain chocolate
- 50 g/2 oz/2 squares white chocolate
- 30 ml/2 tbsp/2 tbsp liquid glucose
- pink paste food colouring

1 Preheat the oven to 150°C/300°F/Gas 2. Grease and line the base of the pudding basin (bowl) with a circle of greaseproof (wax) paper. Cream together the butter or margarine and brown sugar. Gradually add the eggs with a little of the flour to prevent curdling. Sieve (sift) the remaining flour and spice and add to the bowl. Stir in the mixed fruit and nuts and turn into the prepared basin or bowl. Level the surface and bake for 1¹/2 hours or until a skewer inserted into the centre of the cake comes out clean. Allow to cool completely.

2 To make the chocolate moulding icing, break up the chocolate and place in a bowl with the glucose over a pan of hot water. Leave until melted, cool slightly then add the egg white. Gradually add the icing (confectioners) sugar, beating well after each addition, until too stiff to manage. Turn out onto a flat surface and knead in the remaining sugar until stiff.

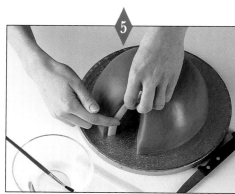

3 To make the modelling paste, melt the plain (semisweet) and white chocolate in separate bowls. Add half the glucose to the plain chocolate and stir until a stiff paste is formed. Wrap tightly. Add some pink food colouring and the remaining glucose to the white chocolate and mix to a paste. Chill both pastes until firm.

4 Cut a triangular wedge out of the cake, place the cake on the board and brush all over with apricot glaze. Roll out the marzipan on a surface dusted with icing (confectioners) sugar and cover the cake, tucking the paste into the cut section to maintain the cut-out shape. Trim off the excess marzipan around the base.

5 Roll out the chocolate moulding icing on a surface dusted with cornflour (cornstarch) and use to cover the cake in the same way. Cut two thin strips from the marzipan trimmings. Dampen the undersides with water and position inside the cut-out wedge to resemble marzipan layer.

6 *Thin a little brown food colouring with water. Dip the sponge in the colour and stipple the surface of the icing. Leave to dry.*

7 Lightly knead two-thirds of the modelling paste and shape into 18 small eggs. Cover some with gold foil. Position the eggs inside the cut-out wedge.

Thinly roll out the remaining modelling paste and cut 2 cm/³/₄ in wide strips from the dark paste and 5 mm/¹/₄ in wide strips from the pink paste. Dampen the undersides of the pink paste and lay over the dark. Cut two 13 cm/5 in strips, press the ends together to make loops and secure to the cake. Secure two 7.5 cm/3 in strips for ribbon ends and cover the centre with another small strip. (Place a piece of crumpled foil under each strip until hardened.)

GHOST

This children's cake is really simple to make yet very effective. Use an 18 cm/7 in square cake of your choice, such as a citrus- or chocolate-flavoured Madeira, or a light fruit cake.

INGREDIENTS

Serves 14
- 4-egg quantity orange-flavoured quick-mix sponge cake
- 900 g/2 lb/2 lb sugarpaste (fondant) icing
- black food colouring
- 350 g/12 oz/³/₄ lb butter icing
- cornflour (cornstarch) for dusting

MATERIALS AND EQUIPMENT

- 18 cm/7 in square cake tin (pan)
- greaseproof (wax) paper
- 300 ml/¹/₂ pt/1 ¹/₄ cup pudding basin (bowl)
- 23 cm/9 in round cakeboard
- palette knife (spatula)
- fine paintbrush

STORING

The iced cake can be covered loosely in foil and stored in a cool, dry place for up to two weeks.

FREEZING

The sponge can be frozen for up to two months.

1 Preheat the oven to 150°C/300°F/Gas 2. Grease and line the base of cake tin with greased greaseproof (wax) paper. Grease and line the base of pudding basin (bowl) with greaseproof (wax) paper. Half-fill the basin with cake mixture and turn the remainder into the cake tin (pan). Bake the basin for 25 minutes and the tin for 1¹/₂ hours. Allow to cool.

2 Knead a little black food colouring into 125 g/4 oz/¹/₄ lb of the sugarpaste (fondant) icing and use to cover the cakeboard. Trim off the excess.

3 Cut two small corners off the large cake. Cut two larger wedges off the other two corners. Stand the large cake on the iced board. Halve the larger cake trimmings and wedge around the base of cake.

4 Secure the small cake to the top of the larger cake with a little of the butter icing. Use the remaining butter icing to completely cover the cake.

5 Roll out the remaining sugarpaste (fondant) on a surface dusted with cornflour (cornstarch) to an oval shape about 51 cm/20 in long and 30 cm/12 in wide. Lay over the cake, letting the icing fall into folds around sides. Gently smooth the icing over the top half of the cake and trim off any excess around the base.

6 Using black food colouring and a fine paintbrush, paint two oval eyes onto the head.

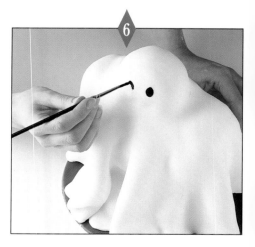

BIRTHDAY BALLOONS

A colourful cake for a child's birthday party, made using either a round sponge cake or fruit cake base.

INGREDIENTS

Serves 18–20

- 20 cm/8 in round sponge or fruit cake, covered with 800 g/1¾ lb/1¾ lb marzipan, if liked
- 900 g/2 lb/2 lb sugarpaste (fondant) icing
- red, green and yellow food colourings
- cornflour (cornstarch), for dusting
- 3 eggs
- 2 egg whites
- 450 g/1 lb/4 cups icing (confectioners) sugar

MATERIALS AND EQUIPMENT

- 25 cm/10 in round silver cakecard
- 3 bamboo skewers, 25 cm/10 in, 24 cm/9½ in and 23 cm/9 in long
- small star cutter
- baking parchment
- greaseproof (wax) paper piping bags
- fine writing nozzle
- 1 m/1 yd fine coloured ribbon
- birthday candles

STORING

The iced cake will keep well in a cool place for up to three weeks.

FREEZING

A fruit cake base can be frozen for up to six months, and a sponge base for up to two months.

Template for the balloon-shaped run-outs; reproduced at actual size.

1 Place the cake on the cakecard. Colour 50 g/2 oz/2 oz of the sugarpaste (fondant) red, 50 g/2 oz/2 oz green and 125 g/4 oz/¼ lb yellow. Roll out the remaining icing on a surface dusted with cornflour (cornstarch) and use to cover the cake. Use 50 g/2 oz/2 oz of the yellow icing to cover the cakecard.

2 Using the tip of a skewer or the end of a paintbrush, make a small hole in the pointed end of one egg. Stir the egg lightly inside then tip out into a bowl. Repeat with the remaining eggs. Carefully wash and dry the shells. (The eggs should be strained before using.)

3 Roll out the red sugarpaste (fondant) icing to about 11 cm/4½ in diameter circle and use to cover one of the egg shells, smoothing to fit around sides and trimming off any excess around the pointed ends. Keep smoothing the icing in the palms of the hands. Push a bamboo skewer up through hole and rest in a tall glass to harden. Repeat on other egg shells with the green and yellow sugarpaste (fondant).

4 Roll out the red, green and yellow trimmings and cut out a small star shape from each. Dampen lightly then thread onto the skewers and secure to the bases of balloons, matching the colours, for the balloon knots.

5 Trace 16 balloon shapes onto a large sheet of baking parchment. Beat the egg whites with the icing (confectioners) sugar until smooth and divide among 4 bowls. Add red colouring to one bowl, green to the second and yellow to the third, leaving the last white. Cover each tightly with cling film (plastic wrap) to prevent a crust forming.

6 Place the white icing in a piping bag fitted with a plain writing nozzle and use to pipe over the traced outlines. Leave to harden slightly. Thin the green icing with a little water until the consistency of pouring cream. Place in a greaseproof (wax) paper piping bag and snip off end. Use to fill a third of the balloon shapes. Repeat with the red and yellow icings. Leave the run-outs for at least 24 hours to harden.

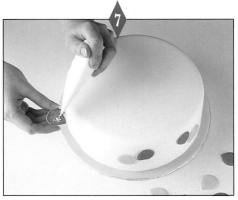

7 Carefully peel the balloons off the baking parchment and secure around the sides of the cake. Pipe strings for the balloons with white icing.

8 Press the large balloons into the top of cake and decorate with the ribbon. Press the candles into the icing around the top edge.

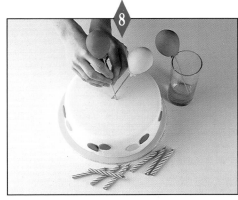

FISH

A very easy, but colourful cake, perfect for a small child's birthday party. Candles can be pressed into the icing covering the board.

INGREDIENTS

Serves 8
- 2-egg quantity quick-mix sponge cake
- 450 g/1 lb/1 lb sugarpaste (fondant) icing
- blue, orange, red, mauve and green food colourings
- cornflour (cornstarch), for dusting
- 350 g/12 oz/¾ lb butter icing
- 1 blue Smartie (M&M)

MATERIALS AND EQUIPMENT

- 3.4 l/6 pt/7½ pt ovenproof mixing bowl
- large oval cakecard or board
- palette knife (spatula)
- 2.5 cm/1 in plain biscuit (cookie) cutter
- greaseproof (wax) paper piping bag

STORING

The iced cake can be covered loosely in foil and stored for up to one week.

FREEZING

The sponge cake can be frozen for up to two months.

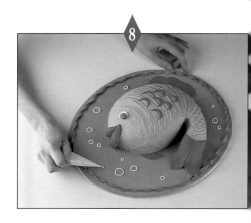

1 Preheat the oven to 170°C/325°F/Gas 3. Grease and line base of the mixing bowl with a circle of greaseproof (wax) paper. Spoon the cake mixture into the prepared bowl, level the surface and bake for 40–50 minutes until just firm, or until a skewer inserted into the middle of the cake comes out clean. Allow to cool.

2 Colour two-thirds of the sugarpaste (fondant) icing blue and roll out very thinly on a surface dusted with cornflour (cornstarch). Lightly dampen the cakecard or board and cover with the sugarpaste (fondant) icing. Trim off excess icing.

3 Invert the cake onto a flat surface and trim to create a fish shape with a curved tail. Using a small knife, trim the edges to give sloping sides. Place on the icing-covered board.

4 Colour all but 15 ml/1 tbsp/1 tbsp of the butter icing orange. Cover the cake completely with the orange butter icing and smooth down with a palette knife (spatula). Score curved lines for scales with the palette knife (spatula), starting from the tail-end and working up towards head.

5 Colour half the remaining sugarpaste (fondant) red. Shape and position two lips. Thinly roll the remainder and cut out the tail and fins. Mark with lines using a knife and position on the fish.

6 Roll a small ball of white sugarpaste (fondant) icing, flatten slightly and position for the eye. Press the blue Smartie (M&M) into centre.

7 Colour a small ball of sugarpaste (fondant) mauve, cut out crescent-shaped scales using a biscuit (cookie) cutter and place on the fish. Colour the remaining sugarpaste (fondant) icing green, roll out and cut long thin strips. Twist each strip and arrange them around board.

8 Place the reserved butter icing in a piping bag and snip off the end. Pipe small circles on the cakeboard around fish for bubbles.

CHRISTMAS CAKE

An unusual Christmas cake which is thoroughly enjoyable to make, provided that you like painting and have a reasonably steady hand.

INGREDIENTS

Serves 35
- 25 cm/10 in round rich fruit cake, covered with 1.1 kg/2½ lb/2½ lb marzipan
- 1.4 kg/3 lb/3 lb sugarpaste (fondant) icing
- cornflour (cornstarch), for dusting
- red, yellow, green and mauve food colourings

MATERIALS AND EQUIPMENT

- 33 cm/13 in round gold cakeboard
- baking parchment
- dressmakers' pins
- fine paintbrush
- 1 m/1 yd × 2.5 cm/1 in wide red ribbon
- red candle

STORING

The iced cake can be wrapped loosely in foil and stored in a cool place for up to one month.

FREEZING

The fruit cake base can be frozen for up to six months.

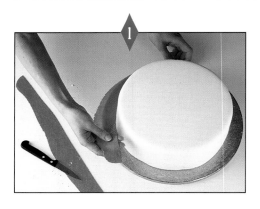

1 Place the cake on the board. Reserve 125 g/4 oz/¼ lb of the sugarpaste (fondant) icing and use the remainder to cover the cake. Colour the reserved sugarpaste (fondant) red and roll out thinly on a surface dusted with cornflour (cornstarch). Dampen the surface of the cakeboard and cover with strips of icing. Smooth down gently and trim off the excess around edge of board. Leave for at least 24 hours to harden.

2 Trace the template onto the baking parchment. Make a pin mark in the exact centre of the cake. Lay the template on top of cake so that the apex of the template meets the pin mark. Using a pin, press the template lines onto the surface of the cake so that a faint marking can be seen on the cake. Move the template round and repeat on the remaining three-quarters of the cake.

3 Cut another piece of baking parchment to fit around the circumference of cake and 6.5 cm/2½ in wide. Lay around the sides of the cake so that the base of the template rests on the cakeboard, securing the ends with a pin. Using a pin, mark a line onto the icing around the top edge of the template. Cut the template in half lengthways and reposition around the cake as before. Mark another line around the top edge of the template, halfway down the sides of the cake. Remove the template.

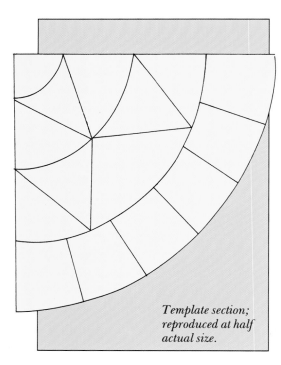

Template section; reproduced at half actual size.

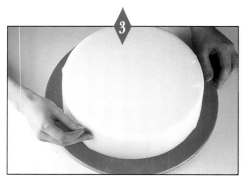

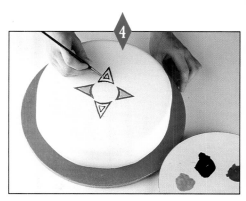

4 Place a little red, yellow, green and mauve food colourings onto a large flat plate and thin each with a little water, as if on a painter's palette. Paint a red triangle of icing onto the cake next to the central circle to within 1 mm/^{1}/$_{16}$ in of the template markings. Paint another triangle opposite the first. Fill in the centres with yellow. Use the green and mauve colours to fill the remaining triangles around the central circle.

5 Using a clean paintbrush dampened with water, lightly 'smudge' the red and yellow colours together. Repeat on the green and mauve triangles.

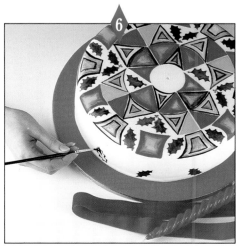

6 Using this technique, build up a design over the top and sides of the cake, creating a random design or following the photographed cake. Leave the area between the two marked lines around the cake blank for the ribbon. Incorporate a holly leaf at intervals around the cake, first painting an outline and then filling in with colour. Finish the leaves with red berries.

7 Secure the ribbon around cake and place a candle in the centre, using a little icing (confectioners) sugar mixed to a paste with water as glue.

ARTIST'S BOX AND PALETTE

Making cakes is an art in itself, and this cake proves it. It is the perfect celebration cake for any artist of any age.

INGREDIENTS

Serves 30
- 20 cm/8 in square rich fruit cake
- 45 ml/3 tbsp/3 tbsp apricot glaze
- 450 g/1 lb/1 lb marzipan
- 800 g/1¾ lb/1¾ lb sugarpaste (fondant) icing
- 125 g/4 oz/⅓ cup royal icing, for fixing
- chestnut, blue, mulberry, yellow, green, black, silver and paprika food colourings

MATERIALS AND EQUIPMENT

- stiff paper for template
- greaseproof (wax) paper
- 25–26 cm/10 in square cakeboard
- fine paintbrush

STORING

The iced cake can be stored in an airtight container for up to three weeks.

FREEZING

Not recommended.

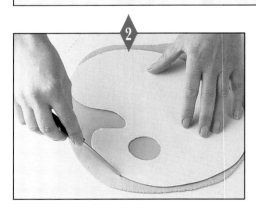

1 Brush the cake with the apricot glaze. Roll out the marzipan, cover the cake and leave to dry for 12 hours.

2 Make a template out of stiff paper in the shape of a painter's palette that will fit on top of the cake. Take 175 g/6 oz/6 oz sugarpaste (fondant) and colour a very pale chestnut. Roll out and cut out the palette shape using the template. Place on a sheet of greaseproof (wax) paper and leave to dry for 12 hours.

3 Take 450 g/1 lb/1 lb sugarpaste (fondant) icing and colour brown with the chestnut colouring. Roll this out, brush the marzipanned cake with a little water to slightly dampen, and cover the cake with the brown-coloured sugarpaste (fondant) icing, cutting away any surplus. Position the cake on the cakeboard, securing underneath with a dab of royal icing. Leave to dry for several hours.

4 Take the remaining 175 g/6 oz/6 oz of the sugarpaste (fondant) icing. Leave half white, divide the remainder into seven equal parts and colour yellow, blue, black, silver, paprika, green and mulberry. Shape the box handle and clips with black and silver and leave to dry on greaseproof (wax) paper for several hours. Shape the paintbrush bristles from paprika-coloured sugarpaste and mark the hairs of the bristles with a knife. Shape the paintbrush handles in various colours and attach the handles, silver metal parts and bristles with a little royal icing. Leave to dry on greaseproof (wax) paper for several hours.

5 Shape the paint tubes from small oblongs of white rolled-out sugarpaste (fondant) icing, sealing the edges with a little water.

6 Paint on markings with a fine paintbrush. Shape squeezed-out paint in various colours and attach two to the paint tubes with a little royal icing. Leave all to dry on greaseproof (wax) paper for several hours.

7 Roll out two small rectangles of any remaining white sugarpaste (fondant) icing to represent sheets of paper, and with a paintbrush and watered down food colours, brush on patterns. Leave to dry on greaseproof (wax) paper for several hours.

8 Using a fine paintbrush, paint wood markings onto the box.

9 To assemble, using a little royal icing, attach the handle and clips onto the front side of the box, and the palette to the top of the cake. Position the paintbrushes, paint tubes, squeezed-out paint and painted paper on the cake and around the board.

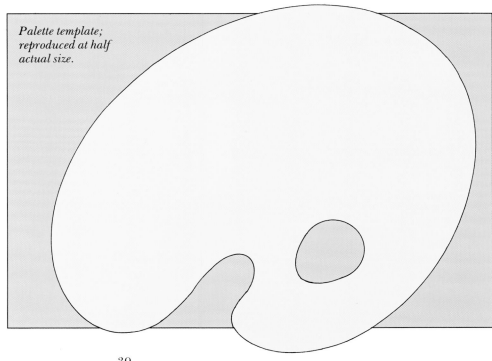

Palette template; reproduced at half actual size.

LIQUORICE SWEET (CANDY) CAKE

If liquorice sweets (candies) are a favourite, this is a cake to fantasize over. Larger than lifesize, its base is a square Madeira cake filled with butter icing, and topped with a pile of smaller look-alike liquorice sweets (candies).

INGREDIENTS

Serves 15–20
- 20 cm/8 in square Madeira cake
- 15 cm/6 in square Madeira cake
- 675 g/1½ lb/1½ lb butter icing
- 45 ml/3 tbsp/3 tbsp apricot glaze
- 350 g/12 oz/¾ lb marzipan
- 800 g/1¾ lb/1¾ lb sugarpaste (fondant) icing
- egg-yellow, black, blue, mulberry food colourings

MATERIALS AND EQUIPMENT

- 25 cm/10 in square cakeboard
- 4.5 cm/1¾ in round cutter

STORING

Kept in an airtight container, the cake will stay fresh for up to three days.

FREEZING

Not recommended.

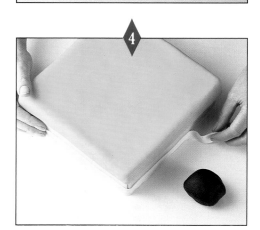

1 Cut both the cakes horizontally into three. Fill with the butter icing, reserving a little to coat the outsides of the smaller cake. Wrap and set aside the smaller cake.

2 Brush the 20 cm/8 in cake with the apricot glaze. Roll out the marzipan and cover the cake. Position the cake on the cakeboard, securing underneath with a little butter icing. Leave to dry for 12 hours.

3 Take 350 g/12 oz/¾ lb of the sugarpaste (fondant) and colour yellow. Take 125 g/4 oz/¼ lb of the sugarpaste (fondant) and colour half black and leave the other half white. Brush the marzipanned cake lightly with water. Roll out the yellow icing; cover the top and down one third of the sides of the cake.

4 Roll out the white icing to a strip wide and long enough to cover the sides of the bottom one-third of the cake. Position onto the cake, securing the join with a little water. Roll out the black icing to a strip wide enough and long enough to fill the central third strip, between the yellow and white strips. Position onto the cake.

5 Take the 15 cm/6 in cake. Cut into three equal strips. Divide two of the strips each into three squares. From the remaining strip cut out two circles (about 4.5 cm/1¾ in), using a cutter as a guide.

6 Take another 100 g/4 oz/¼ lb sugarpaste (fondant) and colour it black. Take the remaining 225 g/8 oz/½ lb sugarpaste (fondant) and divide into four equal amounts: colour blue, pink, yellow and leave one portion white.

7 Coat the outsides of the cut-out cake pieces with the reserved butter icing. Make the square liquorice sweets (candies) for the top of the cake using the coloured icings, rolling out strips for the sides and squares to coat the tops. Secure any of the strip joins with a little water.

8 Make small balls of pink and blue icing for the round sweets (candies), attaching them by lightly pressing into the butter icing.

9 To make the small rolls for the edges of the cake, roll out any black sugarpaste (fondant) trimmings into a strip about 18 × 13 cm/7 × 5 in. With your fingers, roll out 18 cm/7 in long sausage shapes of yellow, pink, white and blue icing. Position one of the colours down the length of the black strip, roll over to form a filled roll, securing the join underneath with water. Slice into three across. Repeat with the remaining colours.

10 Arrange the smaller liquorice allsorts in a pile on top and around the edges of the large cake.

CANDLE CAKE

Marbled icing is so effective that little other decoration is required. This design combines blue and orange but any other strong colour combination is equally effective.

INGREDIENTS

Serves 20
- 20 cm/8 in round rich fruit cake, covered with 800 g/1¾ lb/1¾ lb marzipan
- 900 g/2 lb/2 lb sugarpaste (fondant) icing
- blue, green and orange food colourings
- cornflour (cornstarch), for dusting

MATERIALS AND EQUIPMENT

- 25 cm/10 in round silver cakecard
- 1 bamboo skewer
- 2 household candles
- cling film (plastic wrap)

STORING

The iced cake can be wrapped loosely in foil and stored in a cool place for up to four weeks.

FREEZING

The fruit cake base can be frozen for up to six months.

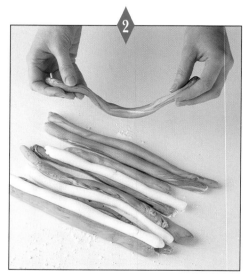

1 Place the cake on the card. Colour 125 g/4 oz/¼ lb of the sugarpaste (fondant) icing orange and reserve. Reserve another 125 g/4 oz/¼ lb of white sugarpaste (fondant). Divide the remaining icing into three parts. Knead the orange colouring into one piece until deep orange but still streaked with colour. Knead a mixture of blue and green colour into another piece until streaky. Leave the remaining piece white.

2 Lightly dust the work surface with the cornflour (cornstarch). Roll long sausages of icing in the three colours and lay on the work surface.

3 Twist the colours together and knead for several seconds until the strips of colour are secured together but retain their individual colours.

4 Roll out the marbled icing and use to cover the cake, trimming off the excess around the base.

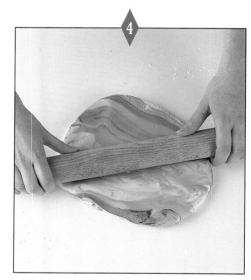

5 Take a small piece of the reserved orange sugarpaste (fondant), about the size of a large grape, and shape into a candle flame. Thread onto the end of the bamboo skewer. Thinly roll the remaining orange sugarpaste (fondant) and use to cover the card around cake. Re-roll the trimmings and cut another strip, 1 cm/½ in wide. Secure over the orange icing around the cake. Cut another strip, 5 mm/¼ in wide, and use to complete the border.

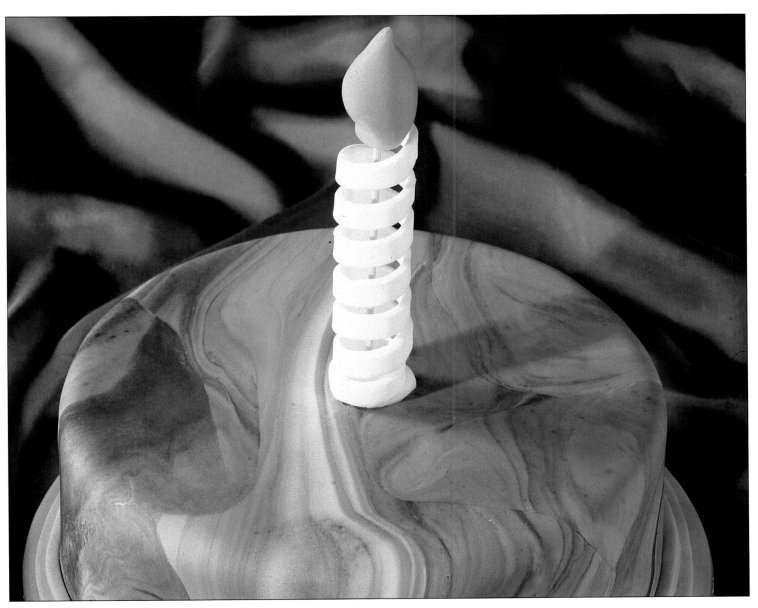

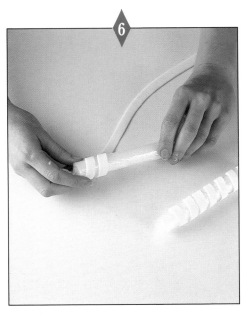

6 *Wrap the candles in cling film (plastic wrap), twisting ends together. (One candle is prepared as a spare.) Roll the reserved white sugarpaste (fondant) to a long thin strip cut vertically into two sections, each about 5 mm/¼ in wide. Starting from one end of a covered candle, coil the icing around the candle, trimming off any excess icing at end. Leave for at least 48 hours to harden.*

7 *To release the icing, untwist the cling film (plastic wrap) and gently push out the candle inside. Carefully peel away the cling film (plastic wrap).*

8 *Place a dot of white icing in the centre of the cake and use to secure the icing candle. Push the bamboo skewer down through the centre to finish.*

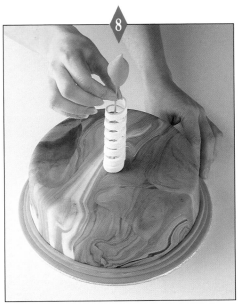

INDIAN ELEPHANT

This is a cake to say happy birthday to children and adults alike. Be as colourful as you like when decorating the elephant – dress it up for a very special occasion.

INGREDIENTS

Serves 30
- 30 cm/12 in square Madeira cake
- 675 g/1½ lb/1½ lb butter icing
- 225 g/8 oz/½ lb marzipan
- black, holly green, mint green, yellow, mulberry food colourings
- chocolate coins, silver balls, coloured chocolate buttons, white chocolate buttons, liquorice allsorts (candy), Smartie (M&M)
- 125 g/4 oz/¼ lb desiccated (shredded) coconut
- 30 ml/2 tbsp/2 tbsp apricot glaze

MATERIALS AND EQUIPMENT

- stiff paper for template
- 36 cm/14 in square cakeboard
- cocktail stick (or toothpick)

STORING

Kept in an airtight container, the cake will stay fresh for up to three days.

FREEZING

Not recommended.

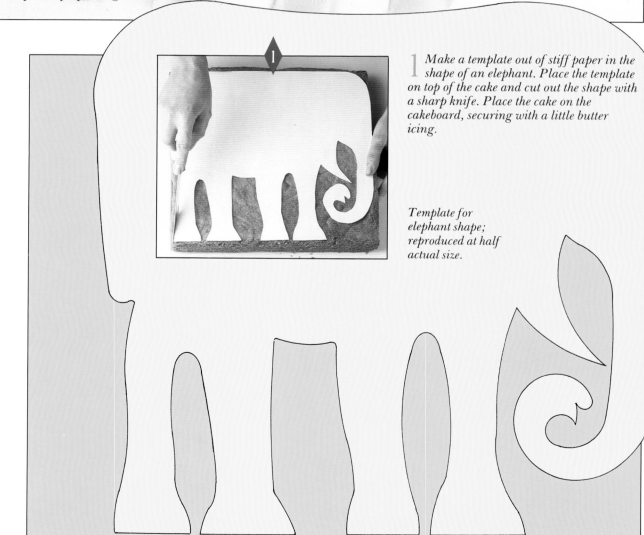

1 Make a template out of stiff paper in the shape of an elephant. Place the template on top of the cake and cut out the shape with a sharp knife. Place the cake on the cakeboard, securing with a little butter icing.

Template for elephant shape; reproduced at half actual size.

2 *Colour the remaining butter icing pale grey, using the black food colour. Cover the top and sides of the cake with the icing carefully, so as not to loosen the cake crumbs. Swirl with a palette knife (spatula).*

3 *Using a cocktail stick dipped in black food colour, swirl in black highlights.*

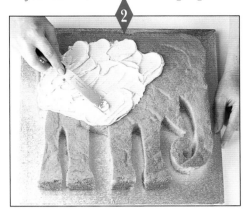

4 *Taking half of the marzipan, roll out and cut out shapes for the elephant's tusk, headpiece and blanket. Place them in position on the cake. Colour the remaining marzipan pink, yellow and holly green. Roll out and cut out patterns for the blanket, headpiece, trunk and tail. Roll small balls of yellow and pink to make the ankle bracelets.*

5 *Place all in position to decorate the elephant, along with the coins, silver balls, chocolate buttons (using the white ones, halved for the toe nails) and a liquorice allsort and Smartie (M&M) for the eye.*

6 *Rub a little mint green food colour into the coconut with your fingers until well mixed, to represent grass. Brush any uncovered cakeboard with a little apricot glaze and sprinkle the coconut over, in and around the elephant, carefully so as not to touch the icing.*

CHRISTMAS CRACKER

A festive cake that is fun to make and fun to eat. To make sure it is really fresh for your Christmas party, the cake can be made and decorated a day or two ahead of time, then simply cut it in half and arrange on the cakeboard with the colourful decorations to serve.

INGREDIENTS

Serves 8
- 4-egg quantity whisked sponge cake
- 225 g/8 oz/½ lb jam, for filling
- 30 ml/2 tbsp/2 tbsp apricot glaze
- 625 g/1 lb 6 oz/1 lb 6 oz sugarpaste (fondant) icing
- Christmas red, mint green, yellow, black, blue food colouring
- red, gold and green foil-wrapped chocolate eggs, coins and bars

MATERIALS AND EQUIPMENT

- 33 × 23 cm/13 × 9 in Swiss (jelly) roll tin (pan)
- 2 small red candles
- 32–36 cm/13–14 in cakeboard

STORING

Kept in an airtight container, the cake will stay fresh for up to three days.

FREEZING

Not recommended.

1 Preheat the oven to 180°C/350°F/Gas 4. Grease and line a 33 × 23 cm/13 × 9 in Swiss (jelly) roll tin (pan). Spoon the cake mixture into the prepared tin (pan) and bake in the preheated oven for 20–25 minutes. Allow to cool, spread with the jam and make into a roll. Cut 2.5 cm/1 in off each end of the Swiss (jelly) roll. Cut each piece in half. Set aside. Brush the outside of the roll with the apricot glaze.

2 Take 450 g/1 lb sugarpaste (fondant) and colour it red. Roll it out so it is 15 cm/6 in longer than the length of the trimmed cake, and wide enough to wrap around it. Position the cake in the centre of the red sugarpaste (fondant) icing and wrap around to cover, keeping the join underneath. Secure with water and trim where necessary.

3 Pinch the icing slightly where it meets the ends of the cake to resemble a cracker, and place the reserved pieces of cake inside each end of the icing to support them. Using any red icing trimmings, cut out two circles the same diameter as the ends of the cracker. Dampen the edges and position one at each end of the cracker, pressing together to seal.

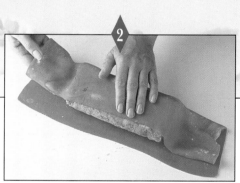

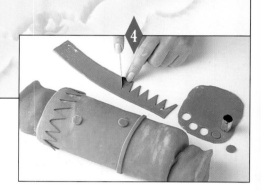

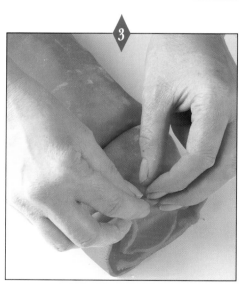

4 Use the remaining icing as follows: colour most of it green and yellow for the decorations, leave a little white for the snowman, and colour a very small amount black and blue. Roll out the green and yellow icing. Cut strips with a knife and small circles with a small cutter or end of a large piping nozzle to decorate the cracker. Arrange the decorations on the cracker, securing with a little water.

5 Make the snowman with the white icing. Shape the body, head, arms and legs separately, then attach to the body, securing with a little water. Shape the hat, eyes and mouth from the black icing, the bow tie from the green, buttons from the red, and a nose from the blue. Position these on the snowman, securing with a little water. Press two small red candles into his arms to hold. Leave to set.

6 When ready to serve, cut the cake in half, making jagged edges, and position on the cakeboard. Sit the snowman on top of one half and arrange the wrapped sweets around the board.

TERRACOTTA FLOWERPOT

A cake ideal for celebrating a gardener's birthday, Mother's Day or a Happy Retirement. The cake is baked in a pudding basin (deep bowl) for the flowerpot shape and filled with a colourful arrangement of icing flowers and foliage.

INGREDIENTS

Serves 15
- 3-egg quantity Madeira cake mixture
- 175 g/6 oz/6 oz jam
- 175 g/6 oz/6 oz butter icing
- 30 ml/2 tbsp/2 tbsp apricot glaze
- 575 g/1¼ lb/1¼ lb sugarpaste (fondant) icing
- 125 g/4 oz/⅓ cup royal icing, for fixing
- dark orange-red, black, red, silver, green, purple, yellow food colouring
- 2 chocolate-flake bars, coarsely crushed

MATERIALS AND EQUIPMENT

- 1.1 l/2 pt/5 cup pudding basin (deep bowl)
- greaseproof (wax) paper
- string
- fine paintbrush
- thin green wire
- 23 cm/9 in round cakeboard

STORING

Kept in an airtight container, the cake will stay fresh for up to three days.

FREEZING

Not recommended.

1 Preheat the oven to 160°C/325°F/Gas 3. Grease and line the bottom of a 1.1 l/2 pt/5 cup pudding basin (deep bowl). Spoon in the cake mixture and bake for 1¼ hours. Cover with foil for last 10 minutes if the top begins to brown. Turn out and cool on a wire rack.

2 When cold trim the top of the cake flat if it has domed. Cut the cake horizontally into three, and fill with the jam and butter icing.

3 Cut out a shallow circle from the top of the cake, leaving a 1 cm/½ in rim round the edge.

4 Brush the outside of the cake and the rim with the apricot glaze. Take 400 g/14 oz/scant 1 lb of the sugarpaste (fondant) icing and colour deep orange-red. Measure round the cake at its widest part and its height, with string. Roll out the deep orange-red-coloured icing to this measurement, remembering to add the width of the rim to the height. Wrap the icing round the cake and over the rim, moulding gently with your hands to fit. Reserve the trimmings, wrapped. Leave the cake to dry for several hours.

5 Using the trimmings, shape the decorations and handles for the flowerpot. Leave to dry on greaseproof (wax) paper. Sprinkle the flake into the top of the cake to represent soil.

6 Colour a small piece of the remaining sugarpaste (fondant) icing a very pale orange-red, roll out into an oblong and fold over to form a seed bag. Leave to dry then paint on a pattern with a fine paintbrush. Colour a very small piece of icing black and make the seeds. Leave to dry on greaseproof (wax) paper. Colour two more small pieces of icing red and silver and shape the trowel, leaving it to dry over a wooden spoon handle. Colour the remaining icing green, purple and a very small amount yellow.

8 *Shape the leaves and short stems with the green icing using your fingers and mark the veins with the back of a knife. Insert short pieces of thin green wire up some of the stems, so you can create different heights when they go into the flowerpot. Leave to dry over the handle of a wooden spoon. Roll out any remaining green icing and cut to represent grass.*

7 *Shape the flowers with the purple icing by moulding the petals individually and attaching together with royal icing. Roll out the yellow icing and cut out the flower centres with a small knife. Position in the middle of each flower with a small ball of yellow icing, securing with royal icing. Leave to dry on greaseproof (wax) paper.*

9 *Attach the deep orange-red decorations on the flowerpot with royal icing. Arrange the leaves and flowers in the pot. Place on the cakeboard and place the trowel, seed packet and grass around the outside.*

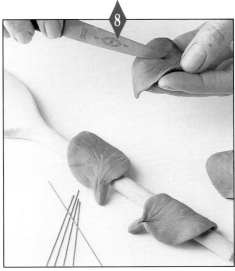

GLITTERING STAR

With a quick flick of a paintbrush you can give a sparkling effect to this glittering cake. Add some shimmering stars and moons and you have a cake ready to celebrate a birthday, Christmas, Halloween or silver wedding anniversary – all for the stars in your life.

INGREDIENTS

Serves 20–25
- 20 cm/8 in round rich fruit cake
- 40 ml/2½ tbsp/2½ tbsp apricot glaze
- 675 g/1½ lb/1½ lb marzipan
- 450 g/1 lb/1 lb sugarpaste (fondant) icing
- 125 g/4 oz/⅓ cup royal icing for fixing
- silver, gold, lilac shimmer, red sparkle, glitter green, primrose sparkle food colourings

MATERIALS AND EQUIPMENT

- greaseproof (wax) paper
- paintbrush
- stiff paper for templates
- 25 cm/10 in round cakeboard or plate

STORING

Kept in an airtight container, the cake will keep for up to three weeks.

FREEZING

Not recommended.

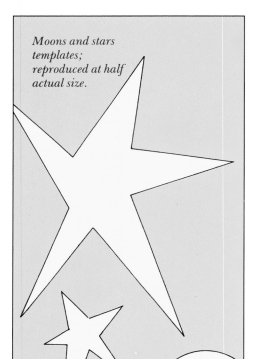

Moons and stars templates; reproduced at half actual size.

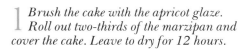

1 Brush the cake with the apricot glaze. Roll out two-thirds of the marzipan and cover the cake. Leave to dry for 12 hours.

2 Roll out the sugarpaste (fondant) icing. Brush the marzipanned cake with a little water to slightly dampen and cover the cake with the sugarpaste (fondant) icing. Leave to dry for several hours.

3 Place the cake on a large sheet of greaseproof (wax) paper. Water down a little powdered silver food colouring and, using a paintbrush loaded with the colour, flick this all over the cake to give a spattered effect. Allow to dry.

4 Make templates out of stiff paper in two or three different-sized moon shapes and three or four irregular star shapes. Take the remaining marzipan, divide into five pieces and colour silver, gold, lilac, pink, green and yellow. Roll out each colour and cut into stars and moons using the templates as a guide, cutting some of the stars in half.

5 Place the cut-out shapes on the greaseproof (wax) paper, brush each with its own colour in powdered form to add more glitter. Allow to dry for several hours.

6 Position the cake on the cakeboard, securing underneath with a dab of royal icing, or place on a plate. Arrange the stars and moons at different angles all over the cake, attaching with royal icing, and position the halved stars upright as though coming out of the cake. Allow to set.

PORCUPINE

Melt-in-the-mouth strips of flaky chocolate bars give this porcupine its spiky coating, and a quick-mix moist chocolate cake makes the base. It's a fun cake for a children's or adults' party.

INGREDIENTS

Serves 15
- 3-egg quantity chocolate-flavoured quick-mix sponge cake
- 575 g/1¼ lb/1¼ lb chocolate-flavoured butter icing
- 50 g/2 oz/2 oz white marzipan
- cream, black, green, red, brown food colourings
- 5–6 chocolate flake bars

MATERIALS AND EQUIPMENT

- greaseproof (wax) paper
- 1.1 l/2 pt/5 cup pudding basin (deep bowl)
- 600 ml/1 pt/2½ cup pudding basin (deep bowl)
- 36 cm/14 in long rectangular cakeboard
- cocktail stick (or toothpick)
- fine paintbrush

STORING

Kept in a container in the refrigerator, the cake will stay fresh for up to three days.

FREEZING

Not recommended.

1 Preheat the oven to 160°C/325°F/Gas 3. Grease and line the bottoms of a 1.1 l/2 pt/5 cup and a 600 ml/1 pt/2½ cup pudding basin (deep bowl). Spoon the cake mixture into both basins (bowls) to two-thirds full. Bake in the preheated oven, allowing 55 mins–1 hr for the larger basin (bowl) and 35–40 mins for the smaller basin (bowl). Turn out and allow to cool on a wire rack.

2 Place both cakes on a surface so the widest ends are underneath. Take the smaller cake and, holding a sharp knife at an angle, slice off a piece from either side to create a pointed nose at one end.

3 Place the larger cake on the cakeboard behind the smaller one. Cut one of the cut-off slices in half and position either side, between the larger and small cake, to fill in the side gaps. Place the other cut-off piece on top to fill in the top gap, securing all with a little butter icing.

4 Spread the remaining butter icing all over the cake. On the pointed face part, make markings with a cocktail stick.

5 Break or cut the flake bars into thin strips and stick into the butter icing over the body of the porcupine to represent spikes.

6 Reserve a small portion of marzipan. Divide the remainder into three and colour one portion black, one green and one cream. Colour a tiny portion of the reserved, white marzipan brown for the apple stems. With the cream marzipan shape the ears and feet, using black and white make the eyes, and with the rest of the black shape the nose and the claws for the feet. With the green marzipan make the apples, painting on red markings with a fine paintbrush. Position the stems. Place everything except the apples in its proper place on the porcupine cake. Finally, place the apples on the board by the front of the porcupine.

TROPICAL PARROT

Create a tropical feel to any celebration with this colourful, exotic cake, whether for a Bon Voyage to faraway places or a simple birthday. The cake is made from one round Madeira cake, cutting out three easy shapes to give the parrot's body, tail and the branch it sits on. You can then be as decorative as you like with the markings and foliage.

INGREDIENTS

Serves 15
- *20 cm/8 in round Madeira cake*
- *500 g/1 lb 2 oz/1 lb 2 oz butter icing*
- *450 g/1 lb/1 lb sugarpaste (fondant) icing*
- *red, brown, green, yellow, orange, blue, purple, pink, black food colouring*

MATERIALS AND EQUIPMENT

- *20 cm/8 in round cake tin (pan)*
- *greaseproof (wax) paper*
- *stiff paper for templates*
- *36 cm/14 in square cakeboard*

STORING

Kept in an airtight container, the cake will stay fresh for up to three days.

FREEZING

Not recommended.

1 *Make templates out of stiff paper for the parrot's body, tail and branch. Place the templates on top of the cake and cut out the shapes with a sharp knife.*

2 *Take the sugarpaste (fondant) icing and colour about one-third red. Colour a quarter of the remaining piece brown and the rest yellow, pink, orange, blue, purple, black, green and light green. Leave a small amount white.*

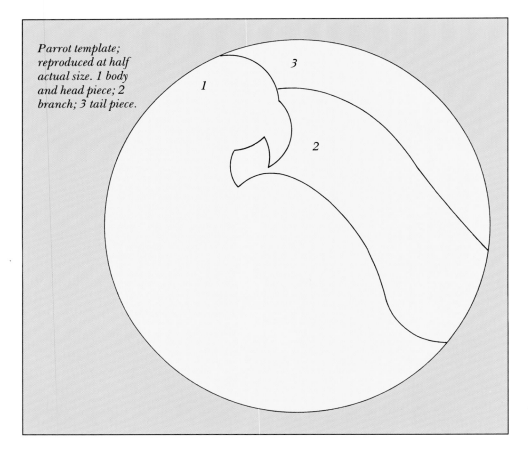

Parrot template; reproduced at half actual size. 1 body and head piece; 2 branch; 3 tail piece.

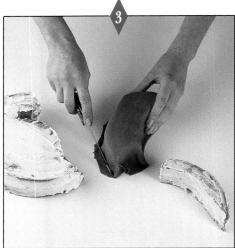

3 *Slice each piece of cake (body, tail and branch) in half horizontally and fill with some of the butter icing. Use the remaining butter icing to coat the outsides of the cake. Measure the length and depth of the cake which forms the branch. Roll out the brown icing in one piece large enough to cover it. Position over the cake branch and trim to fit.*

4 Measure the length and depth of the sides of the parrot's body. Roll out some of the red icing and cut strips to match the measurements. Press onto the butter icing to fix in position. Roll out a piece of red icing for the top of the parrot's body, using the template as a guide. Leave out the face, beak and blue body parts. Position the red sugarpaste (fondant) on the butter icing, reserving the trimmings. Roll out a piece of white and some black icing for the face and beak, cut to fit and ease into position with your fingers. Do the same with a piece of blue icing to finish off the body, and with the tailpiece, using the rest of the reserved red icing.

5 Roll out the other coloured pieces of icing. Cut out pieces in the shape of feathers, some with jagged edges. Press these into position on the body and tail, easing to fit with your fingers. Secure with a little water, bending and twisting some of the 'feathers' to create different angles and heights. Cut out leaf and flower shapes for the branch out of the green and pink icings. Use templates as a guide, if wished.

6 Place the iced parrot pieces in position on the cakeboard. Make the eye for the parrot. Secure the eye onto the head with water, and use water to fix leaves and flower on the branch. If wished, colour an additional 125 g/4 oz/1/4 lb sugarpaste (fondant) icing green. Roll and cut out more leaves to decorate the base of the parrot.

HALLOWEEN PUMPKIN

Halloween is a time for spooky cakes – witches may even burst out of them. This one is made in two pudding basins (deep bowls), making it easy to create a pumpkin effect. Make the cake and icing with your favourite flavour – and you are all set for a party full of eerie surprises.

INGREDIENTS

Serves 15

- 3-egg quantity orange-flavoured Madeira cake mixture
- 250 g/9 oz/9 oz orange-flavoured butter icing
- 450 g/1 lb/1 lb sugarpaste (fondant) icing
- 125 g/4 oz/¼ lb royal icing for fixing
- orange, black, yellow food colourings

MATERIALS AND EQUIPMENT

- greaseproof (wax) paper
- 2 × 1.1 l/2 pt/5 cup pudding basins (deep bowls)
- thin wooden skewer
- thin paintbrush
- 23 cm/9 in round cakeboard

STORING

Kept in an airtight container, the cake will stay fresh for up to three days.

FREEZING

Not recommended.

1 Preheat the oven to 160°C/325°F/Gas 3. Grease and line the bottoms of two 1.1 l/2 pt/5 cup pudding basins (deep bowls). Divide the cake mixture equally between them and bake for 1¼ hours. Turn out and cool on a wire rack.

2 Trim the widest ends of each cake so they will fit flat against one another to make a round shape. Split each cake in half horizontally and fill with some of the butter icing, then stick the two cakes together with butter icing to form a pumpkin. Trim one of the narrow ends off slightly, to give a better shape. Let this end be the bottom of the pumpkin. Cover the outside of the cake with the remaining butter icing.

3 Take 350 g/12 oz/¾ lb of the sugarpaste (fondant) icing and colour it orange. Roll out to cover the cake, trimming to fit where necessary. Mould it gently with your hands to give a smooth surface. Reserve the trimmings.

4 With a thin wooden skewer, mark the segments onto the pumpkin. With a fine paintbrush and watered-down orange food colouring, paint on the markings for the pumpkin flesh. Use orange sugarpaste (fondant) trimmings for the top of the cake where the witch bursts out, by cutting and tearing rolled out pieces to create jagged edges. Attach to the top of the cake with a little water.

5 Take the remaining sugarpaste (fondant) icing and colour three-quarters black. Of the remainder, colour a little yellow and leave the rest white. Use some of the black and white to make the witch, moulding the head, arms and body separately and securing with royal icing. When set, roll out some black icing and cut jagged edges to form a cape. Drape over the arms and body, securing with a little water. Make the hat in two pieces – a circle and a cone – and secure with royal icing. Leave to dry on greaseproof (wax) paper. Shape the cauldron, broomstick and cat's head out of more of the black and yellow icing, securing the handle of the cauldron with royal icing when dry. Leave all to dry completely on greaseproof (wax) paper.

6 Use the remaining black icing for the pumpkin features. Roll out and cut out the eyes, nose and mouth with a sharp knife. Attach to the pumpkin with a little water. Place the cake on the cakeboard, secure the witch on top of the cake with royal icing and arrange the cat, cauldron and broomstick around the base.

CHRISTENING SAMPLER

Instead of embroidering a sampler to welcome a newly-born baby, why not make a sampler cake to celebrate?

INGREDIENTS

Serves 30
- 20 cm/8 in square rich fruit cake
- 45 ml/3 tbsp/3 tbsp apricot glaze
- 450 g/1 lb/1 lb marzipan
- 675 g/1½ lb/1½ lb sugarpaste (fondant) icing
- brown, blue, pink, yellow, orange, green, cream, purple food colourings

MATERIALS AND EQUIPMENT

- 25 cm/10 in square cakeboard
- fine paintbrush
- small heart-shaped biscuit (cookie) cutter

STORING

Kept in an airtight container, the cake will stay fresh for up to three weeks.

FREEZING

Not recommended.

1 Brush the cake with apricot glaze. Roll out the marzipan, cover the cake and leave to dry for 12 hours.

2 Cut 450 g/1 lb/1 lb of the sugarpaste (fondant) icing into three. Take one-third and roll out to the size of the top of the cake. Brush the top of the cake with a little water and cover with the icing.

3 Take the other two-thirds of the icing for the sides and colour brown. Roll out in four separate pieces to the measured length and about 1 cm/½ in wider than the width of each side. Brush each side with a little water, then press each piece of brown icing on, folding over the extra width at the top to represent the edges of a picture frame. Cut off each corner at an angle to represent the mitred join of the frame. Reserve any brown trimmings. Place the cake on the cakeboard.

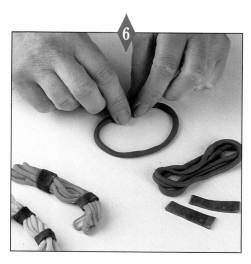

4 With a fine paintbrush, paint over the sides with watered-down brown food colouring to represent wood grain.

5 Take the remaining sugarpaste (fondant) icing and colour small amounts yellow, orange, brown, purple, cream, two shades of blue, green and pink. Leave a little white. Use these colours to shape the ducks, teddy bear, bulrushes, water, apple-blossom branch and leaves. Roll out a small piece of pink icing and cut out a heart with a small heart-shaped biscuit (cookie) cutter (or use a template). Roll out a small piece of white icing and cut out the baby's initial with a small sharp knife.

For the border, roll out strips of blue and yellow icing and cut into oblongs and squares; make small balls and small squares out of the purple icing. For the apple blossom, gently work together the pale pink, deep pink and white sugarpaste (fondant) to give a marbled effect. Shape the flowers from this, placing a small white ball in the centre. Attach all the decorations onto the cake with a little water as you make them.

6 With any leftover colours, roll out long strips of icing with your hands to make 'threads'. Form them into loops, attaching the joins with water. Use small strips of brown icing trimmings to hold the threads together. Arrange around the base of the cake on the board.

MARKET STALL

An open-air market stall is the theme for this cake, bursting with colourful produce. Vary this design if you wish, adding as wide a variety of fruit and vegetables as you wish.

INGREDIENTS

Serves 30
- 20 cm/8 in square rich fruit cake
- 45 ml/3 tbsp/3 tbsp apricot glaze
- 900 g/2 lb/2 lb marzipan
- 450 g/1 lb/1 lb sugarpaste (fondant) icing
- 125 g/4 oz/¼ lb royal icing, for fixing
- brown, green, red, orange, yellow, peach, purple, pink, black food colourings

MATERIALS AND EQUIPMENT

- greaseproof (wax) paper
- 25 cm/10 in square cakeboard
- fine paintbrush

STORING

Kept in an airtight container, the cake will stay fresh for up to three weeks.

FREEZING

Not recommended.

1 Slice 4 cm/1½ in off one side of the cake. Brush the cake with apricot glaze. Take half of the marzipan (reserve the other half for shaping the fruits and vegetables). Roll out three-quarters of it and cover the large piece of cake with it. With the other quarter of marzipan, cover one long side, the top and the two short sides of the cake slice. Leave to dry for 12 hours.

2 Colour half of the sugarpaste (fondant) icing brown and the other half green. Using three-quarters of the brown icing, cover three sides of the large cake (not the cut side), brushing the marzipan first with a little water to secure the icing. With the other quarter of brown icing, cover the marzipanned sides of the smaller piece of cake, measuring first to fit and brushing the marzipan with a little water to stick. Reserve any brown icing trimmings. With these trimmings, roll out and cut narrow dividers to fit the top of the cake. Leave the dividers on greaseproof (wax) paper to dry for several hours.

3 Place the large piece of cake on the cakeboard, with the smaller one in front to create a different level. Attach the cakes together with royal icing and use icing to attach to the board.

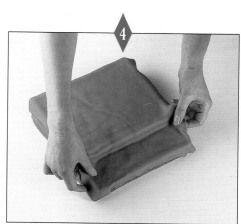

4 Measure the length and width of the cake, including the lower level. Roll out the green icing about 4 cm/1½ in wider and longer than the measured length and width. Brush the marzipan on the tops of the cakes with a little water and cover the cakes with the green icing. Allow it to fall naturally in folds over the edges. Leave the cake to dry for several hours.

5 Take the remaining 450 g/1 lb/1 lb marzipan, reserve a little for the stall holder and colour the rest red, orange, yellow, green, brown, peach and purple. Use these colours to shape the fruits and vegetables. Add markings with a fine paintbrush onto the melons, peaches and potatoes. For the front of the stall, shape baskets and a potato sack out of different shades of brown. For the stallholder, colour the reserved marzipan pink, purple, black and flesh-coloured and shape the head, body and arms separately, attaching with a little royal icing. Make the hands and face features and the hair, and press on with a little water. Place a melon in her arms to hold. Leave all to dry on greaseproof (wax) paper for several hours.

6 Attach the dividers, the baskets and the
  stallholder onto the cake with royal
icing. Arrange the produce in piles on the
stall between the dividers and in the baskets,
and the sack of potatoes in the front.

RACING RING

A simple ring cake makes the perfect base for this teddy-bear racing track. Choose the flattest and widest end of the cake for the top (this will depend on the shape of your ring mould), so there's plenty of room for the icing cars to race around on.

INGREDIENTS

Serves 12
- 2-egg quantity quick-mix sponge cake mixture
- 350 g/12 oz/³/₄ lb butter icing
- 500 g/1 lb 2 oz/1 lb 2 oz sugarpaste (fondant) icing
- 125 g/4 oz/¹/₄ lb royal icing, for fixing
- black, blue, yellow, green, orange, red, purple food colourings
- selection of miniature liquorice sweets (candies), dolly mixtures and teddy bears
- 113 g/4¹/₂ oz packet liquorice Catherine wheels

MATERIALS AND EQUIPMENT

- 22 cm/8¹/₂ in ring mould
- 25 cm/10 in round cakeboard
- 1 thin wooden kebab skewer
- fine paintbrush
- greaseproof (wax) paper

STORING

Kept in an airtight container, the cake will stay fresh for up to three days.

FREEZING

Not recommended.

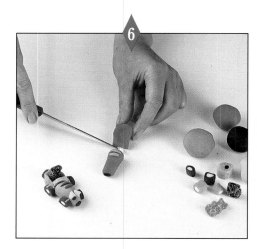

1 Preheat the oven to 160°C/325°F/Gas 3. Spoon the cake mixture into a greased ring mould. Bake for 35–40 minutes. Turn out and cool on a wire rack.

2 Cut the cake in half horizontally and fill with some of the butter icing. Cover the outside of the cake with the remaining butter icing, having the widest part of the cake on top.

3 Cut 350 g/12 oz/³/₄ lb of the sugarpaste (fondant) icing in half. Use half for coating the top and inside ring of the cake and half for coating the outside. To coat the inside of the ring, cut one half of the icing in half again and roll out to the measured diameter and width, (reserve the other piece for the top). Press in position over the butter icing. Roll out the reserved piece for the top to the measured diameter and width (you may find this easier to do in two halves), pressing in position and easing into shape over the butter icing.

4 Take the half piece of icing reserved for coating the outside and roll out to the measured width and diameter. Press in position round the outside of the cake, reserving the white icing trimmings to make the flag. Place the cake on the cakeboard.

5 Take the reserved white icing trimmings and roll out to an oblong for the flag. Cut the wooden kebab skewer to a height of about 12.5 cm/5 in and fold one end of the flag round it, securing with a little water. With black food colouring and a fine paintbrush paint on a chequered pattern. Colour a small piece of icing black, make into a ball and stick on top of the skewer. Create a few folds in the flag and leave to dry on greaseproof (wax) paper.

6 Colour the remaining sugarpaste (fondant) icing blue, yellow, green, orange, red and a very small amount purple. Shape each car in two pieces, attaching in the centre with royal icing where the seat joins the body of the car. Add decorations and headlights and attach dolly mixture wheels with royal icing. Place a candy teddy bear in each car and leave to set.

7 Take the liquorice Catherine wheels and unwind them, removing the centre sweets. Lay the liquorice over the top of the cake to represent the track, leaving a gap in the middle and securing onto the cake with royal icing. Secure one strip round the bottom of the cake also.

8 Cut some of the liquorice into small strips and attach round the middle of the outside of the cake with royal icing. Arrange small liquorice sweets around the bottom of the cake. Position the cars on top of the cake on the tracks and attach the flag to the outside with royal icing.

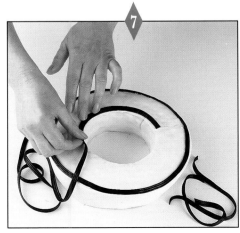

CHOCOLATE FRUIT BIRTHDAY CAKE

A moist chocolate Madeira cake is covered in marzipan and chocolate fudge icing. The fruits are moulded from coloured marzipan and make an eye-catching decoration.

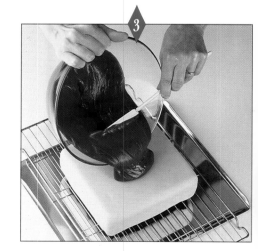

INGREDIENTS

Serves 30

- 18 cm/7 in square deep chocolate-flavoured Madeira cake
- 45 ml/3 tbsp/3 tbsp apricot glaze
- 450 g/1 lb/1 lb homemade or commercial white marzipan
- 450 g/1 lb/1 lb chocolate fudge icing
- red, yellow, orange, green and purple food colouring

DECORATION

- selection of marzipan fruits
- whole cloves
- angelica strips
- 0.75 m/³⁄₄ yd × 1 cm/¹⁄₂ in wide yellow ribbon

MATERIALS AND EQUIPMENT

- greaseproof (wax) paper
- 18 cm/7 in square deep cake tin (pan)
- 20 cm/8 in square silver cakeboard
- wire rack
- nylon piping bag
- medium-sized gateau nozzle

1 Bake the cake and allow to cool on a wire rack. Cut a slice off the top of the cake to level if necessary and invert on to the cakeboard. Brush evenly with apricot glaze.

2 Roll out two-thirds of the marzipan thinly to a 25 cm/10 in square. Place over the cake and smooth the top and down the sides. Trim off the excess marzipan around the base of the cake. Knead the trimmings together and reserve for making the marzipan fruits.

3 Place the cake on a wire rack over a tray and pour the freshly-made chocolate fudge icing over the cake, spreading quickly with a palette knife (metal spatula). Allow the excess icing to fall on the tray. Leave for 10 minutes, then place on to the cakeboard.

4 Using the remaining icing, place in a nylon piping bag fitted with a medium-sized gateau nozzle. Pipe a row of stars around the top edge and base of the cake. Leave to set.

5 Using the reserved marzipan, food colouring, cloves and angelica strips, model a selection of fruits.

6 Measure and fit the ribbon around the side of the cake and secure with a pin. Decorate the top with marzipan fruits.

EIGHTEENTH BIRTHDAY CAKE

A really striking cake for a lucky someone celebrating their eighteenth birthday. Change the shape if you cannot hire the tin (pan).

INGREDIENTS

Serves 80
- 33.5 × 20 cm/13½ × 8 in diamond-shaped deep rich or light fruit cake (make using quantities for a standard 23 cm/9 in round cake)
- 45 ml/3 tbsp/3 tbsp apricot glaze
- 1.1 kg/2½ lb/2½ lb homemade or commercial white marzipan
- 1.6 kg/3½ lb/3½ lbs white sugarpaste (fondant)
- black food colouring
- 30 ml/2 tbsp/2 tbsp royal icing

DECORATION

- 2 m/2 yd × 2.5 cm/1 in wide white ribbon
- ½ m/½ yd × 2 mm/⅛ in wide black ribbon

MATERIALS AND EQUIPMENT

- '18' numeral cutter or template
- greaseproof (wax) paper piping bag
- No. 1 plain writing nozzle

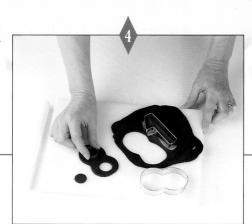

1 Bake the cake and allow to cool. Brush with apricot glaze and place on the cakeboard. Cover with marzipan.

2 Cover the cake using 1.1 kg/2½ lb/2½ lb sugarpaste (fondant). Knead the trimmings into the remaining sugarpaste (fondant) and colour using black food colouring.

3 Roll out two-thirds of the black sugarpaste (fondant) and cut into four strips the width and length of each section of the cakeboard. Brush the board with apricot glaze and place each strip in position; trim to fit neatly.

4 Roll-out one-quarter of the remaining sugarpaste (fondant) and cut out the number '18' using a special biscuit (cookie) cutter or by cutting round a template. Leave on a piece of foam sponge to dry.

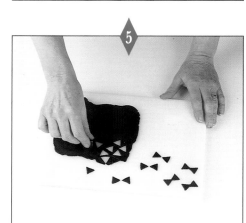

5 Roll out some more icing thinly and cut out 40 triangles for the bow ties and 20 for the wine glasses.

6 Use a tiny round cutter or the end of a plain nozzle to cut out 20 music notes and 10 bases for the glasses, cut in half. Cut out thin strips of icing for the tails of the music notes and the stems of the glasses.

7 Using a greaseproof (wax) paper piping bag fitted with a No. 1 plain writing nozzle, half-fill with royal icing coloured black. Join the bow ties together with tiny beads of icing. Attach the music notes to their tails and the glasses to the stems and bases. Leave them all to dry.

8 Arrange the '18', music notes, wine glasses and bow ties over the top of the cake and attach each with a bead of icing. Continue to fix the decorations onto the sides of the cake.

CHRISTMAS STOCKING CAKE

A bright and happy cake to make for Christmas.
Make the stocking and parcels in advance to save
time at Christmas.

INGREDIENTS

Serves 50

- *20 cm/8 in square rich fruit cake*
- *45 ml/3 tbsp/3 tbsp apricot glaze*
- *900 g/2 lb/2 lb homemade or commercial white marzipan*
- *1.1 kg/2½ lb/2½ lb sugarpaste (fondant) icing*
- *15 ml/1 tbsp/1 tbsp royal icing*
- *red and green food colouring*

DECORATION

- *1¼ m/1¼ yd × 2 cm/¾ in wide red ribbon*
- *1 m/1 yd × 2 cm/¾ in wide green ribbon*

MATERIALS AND EQUIPMENT

- *25 cm/10 in square silver cakeboard*
- *card for template*

1 *Bake the cake and allow to cool. Brush with apricot glaze and place on the cakeboard. Cover the cake with marzipan.*

2 *Reserve 225 g/8 oz/½ lb sugarpaste (fondant) icing for decorations, and use the remainder to cover the cake smoothly. Place the cake in a box and leave to dry in a warm dry place. Measure and fit the red ribbon around the board, securing with a pin, and the green ribbon around the cake, securing with royal icing.*

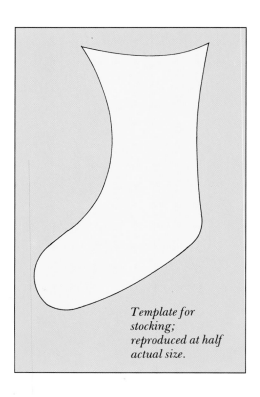

Template for stocking; reproduced at half actual size.

3 *Knead the sugarpaste (fondant) trimmings together. Reserve 125 g/4 oz/¼ lb and cut the remainder in half; colour one half red and the other half green with food colouring. Trace the template of the stocking onto card and cut out. Roll out a piece of white sugarpaste (fondant) and cut out round the template.*

4 *Roll out the red and green sugarpaste (fondant) to 5 mm/¼ in thick and cut each into seven 1 cm/½ in strips. Remove alternate green strips and replace with red strips. Gently roll the stripey sugarpaste (fondant) together.*

5 *Use the template to cut out another stocking shape, allowing an extra 5 mm/¼ in all around.*

6 *Brush the white stocking with apricot glaze and, using a palette knife (metal spatula), lift the striped stocking and place over the white one. Press lightly together and leave to dry.*

7 *Shape the remaining white sugarpaste (fondant) into four parcel shapes and trim each with thin strips of red and green sugarpaste (fondant) ribbons.*

8 Knead the remaining green and red
sugarpaste (fondant) together, keeping
the colours separate. Roll out each into a 20
cm/8 in strip, 1 cm/¹/₂ in wide. Cut each
into two 5 mm/¹/₄ in strips. Pipe a bead of
royal icing on to each corner, press alternate
green and red strips in position and trim to
size. Shape four red and four green balls
and press in position where the sugarpaste
(fondant) strips join, securing with a little
royal icing.

9 Arrange the stocking and parcels in
position on the top of the cake. Leave
to dry.

KULICH

This Russian yeasted cake – Kulich – is known under other names in many Eastern European countries. Traditionally made at Easter time in Slavic countries, this delicious spiced cake was baked in special moulds. For convenience the recipe has been converted for use in either clay flower pots, or coffee tins (cans). Capacity and sizes have been given for both.

INGREDIENTS

Makes 2 cakes
- 15 ml/1 tbsp/1 tbsp dried yeast
- 90 ml/6 tbsp/6 tbsp tepid milk
- 75 g/3 oz/6 tbsp caster (superfine) sugar
- 500 g/1 lb 2 oz/4½ cups plain (all-purpose) flour
- pinch saffron strands
- 30 ml/2 tbsp/2 tbsp dark rum
- 2.5 ml/½ tsp/½ tsp ground cardamom
- 2.5 ml/½ tsp/½ tsp ground cumin
- 50 g/2 oz/¼ cup unsalted butter
- 2 eggs plus 2 egg yolks
- ½ vanilla pod, finely chopped
- 25 g/1 oz/2 tbsp each: chopped mixed candied peel, chopped crystallized ginger, chopped almonds and currants

DECORATION

- 75 g/3 oz/¼ cup icing (confectioners) sugar, sifted
- 7.5–10 ml/1½–2 tsp/1½–2 tsp warm water
- a drop almond essence (extract)
- 2 candles
- blanched almonds
- mixed candied peel

MATERIALS AND EQUIPMENT

- greaseproof (wax) paper
- 2 × 15 cm/6 in clay flower pots or 2 × 500 g/1 lb 2 oz/1⅛ lb coffee tins (cans)

FREEZING

Recommended before the cakes are iced. Wrap and freeze. Defrost and continue.

STORING

Best eaten the day of making.

5 Knock back (punch down) the dough. Divide in two and form each lump into rounds. Press into the prepared pots, cover and leave in a warm place for a further 30 minutes, until the dough comes two-thirds of the way up the sides.

1 Blend the yeast, milk, 25 g/1 oz/2 tbsp sugar and 50 g/2 oz/½ cup flour together, until smooth. Leave in a warm place for 15 minutes, until frothy. Soak the saffron in the rum for 15 minutes.

3 Knead on a lightly floured surface for 5 minutes until smooth and pliable. Place in an oiled bowl, cover and leave to rise in a warm place for 1–1½ hours, until doubled in size.

6 Bake for 35 minutes if using the coffee tins (cans) or 50 minutes if using the clay pots. Test with a skewer and remove from the oven. Transfer to a wire rack and leave to cool.

2 Sift the remaining flour and spices into a bowl and rub in the butter. Stir in the remaining sugar, make a well in the centre and work in the frothed yeast mixture, the saffron liquid and remaining ingredients to form a fine dough.

4 Preheat oven to 190°C/375°F/Gas 5. Grease, base-line and flour the pots or tins (cans).

7 Blend the icing (confectioners) sugar, water and almond essence (extract) together until smooth, to form a thick glacé icing. Pour over the top of each cake, allowing it to drizzle down the sides, and decorate with the candles, nuts and peel.

ST CLEMENTS MARBLED CROWN

A tangy orange-and-lemon marbled cake is transformed into a spectacular centrepiece by the pretty arrangement of fresh flowers in the centre of the ring. The icing is decorated with crystallized fruits, dragées and sugared almonds, creating a dramatic jewelled effect.

INGREDIENTS

Serves 8
- 175 g/6 oz/³⁄4 cup butter
- 75 g/3 oz/good ¹⁄3 cup light soft brown sugar
- 3 eggs, separated
- grated rind and juice 1 orange
- 160 g/5¹⁄2 oz/1¹⁄3 cups self-raising flour
- 75 g/3 oz/6 tbsp caster (superfine) sugar
- grated rind and juice of 1 lemon
- 15 g/¹⁄2 oz/2 tbsp ground almonds
- 350 ml/³⁄4 pt/1 US pt double (heavy) cream
- 15 ml/1 tbsp/1 tbsp Grand Marnier

DECORATION

- 16 crystallized orange and lemon slices
- silver dragées
- 8 gold sugared almonds
- fresh flowers

STORING

Best eaten the day of making.

MATERIALS AND EQUIPMENT

- 850 ml/1¹⁄2 pt/3³⁄4 cups capacity ring mould
- skewer

FREEZING

Recommended at the end of step 5. Wrap and freeze. Defrost at room temperature and ice and decorate.

1 Preheat oven to 180°C/350°F/Gas 4. Grease and flour the mould.

2 Make orange cake mixture. Cream half the butter and the soft brown sugar together until pale and light. Gradually beat in the egg yolks, orange rind and juice until incorporated, and fold in 75 g/3 oz/³⁄4 cup of the flour.

3 Make lemon cake mixture. Cream the remaining butter and caster (superfine) sugar together, stir in the lemon rind and juice and fold in the remaining flour and ground almonds. Whisk the egg whites until stiff, and fold in.

4 Spoon the two mixtures alternately into the prepared tin (pan).

5 Using a skewer or small spoon, swirl through the mixture, to create a marble effect. Bake for 45–50 minutes, until risen and a skewer, inserted into the cake, comes out clean. Cool in the tin (pan) for 10 minutes and transfer to a wire rack to cool completely.

6 Whip the cream and Grand Marnier together until lightly thickened. Spread over the cooled cake and swirl a pattern over the icing.

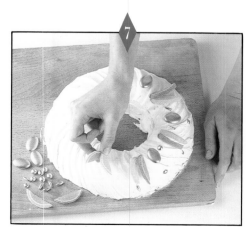

7 Decorate the ring with the crystallized fruits, dragées and almonds to resemble a jewelled crown. Arrange a few pretty, fresh flowers in the centre.

MOTHER'S DAY BASKET

Every mother would love to receive a cake like this on Mother's Day. Choose fresh flowers to decorate the top.

INGREDIENTS	DECORATION	MATERIALS AND EQUIPMENT
Serves 12 • 3-egg quantity of orange-flavoured quick-mix sponge cake • 900 g/2 lb/2 lb orange-flavoured butter icing	• 1 m/1 yd × 1 cm/½ in wide mauve ribbon • ½ m/½ yd × 2 mm/⅛ in wide spotted mauve ribbon • fresh flowers	• 1.1 l/2 pt/5 cup fluted ovenproof glass dish • 15 cm/6 in round silver cakecard • greaseproof (wax) paper piping bags • basket-weave nozzle • kitchen foil

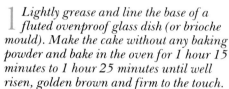

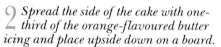

1 Lightly grease and line the base of a fluted ovenproof glass dish (or brioche mould). Make the cake without any baking powder and bake in the oven for 1 hour 15 minutes to 1 hour 25 minutes until well risen, golden brown and firm to the touch.

2 Spread the side of the cake with one-third of the orange-flavoured butter icing and place upside down on a board.

3 Make plenty of greaseproof (wax) paper piping bags and fit with a basket-weave nozzle. Half-fill with butter icing and pipe the sides with a basket-weave pattern (see Basket-weave Wedding Cake).

4 Invert the cake onto the cakecard and spread the top with butter icing. Pipe a shell edging, using the basket-weave nozzle, to neaten the top edge. Continue to pipe the basket-weave icing across the top of the cake, starting at the edge. Leave the cake to set in a cool place.

5 Fold a piece of foil in half, then half again and continue to fold until you have a strip several layers thick.

6 Using the ribbon, bind the strip to cover the foil; bend up the end to secure the ribbon. Bend the foil to make a handle, and press into the icing.

7 Choose some flowers and make a neat arrangement tied with ribbon on top of the cake just before serving. Tie a bow and pin it to the sides of the cake.

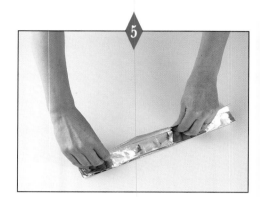

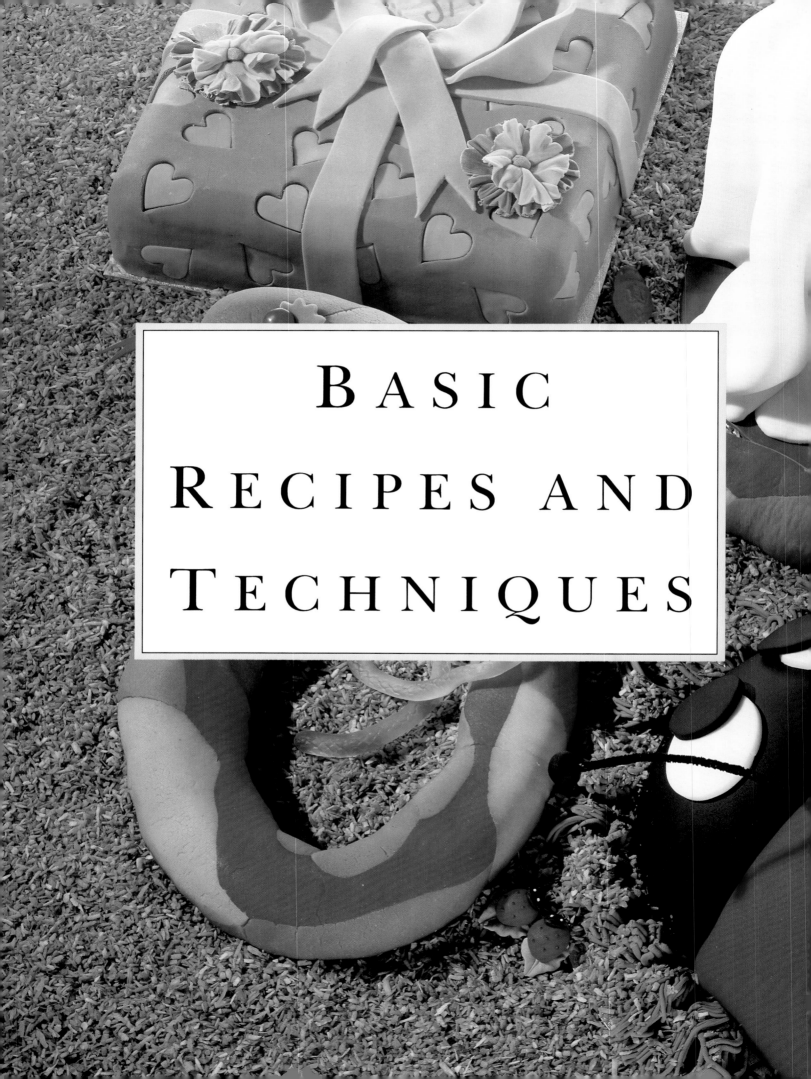

BASIC RECIPES AND TECHNIQUES

BASIC RECIPES & TECHNIQUES

A quick mix sponge cake is light and fluffy; ideal for this springtime cake decorated with lemon butter icing and marzipan flowers.

Quick Mix Sponge Cake

This is a quick-and-easy reliable recipe for making everyday cakes in various sizes, shapes and flavours.

INGREDIENTS	2-EGG QUANTITY	3-EGG QUANTITY	4-EGG QUANTITY
• Self-raising flour	125 g/4 oz/1 cup	175 g/6 oz/1½ cups	225 g/8 oz/2 cups
• Baking powder	5 ml/1 tsp/1 tsp	7.5 ml/1½ tsp/1½ tsp	10 ml/2 tsp/2 tsp
• Caster (superfine) sugar	125 g/4 oz/½ cup	175 g/6 oz/¾ cup	225 g/8 oz/1 cup
• Soft margarine	125 g/4 oz/½ cup	175 g/6 oz/¾ cup	225 g/8 oz/1 cup
• Eggs	2	3	4

1 *Preheat the oven to 170°C/325°F/Gas 3. Prepare the tin (pan) according to the recipe.*

2 *Sift the flour and baking powder into a bowl. Add sugar, margarine and eggs. Mix together with a wooden spoon, then beat for 1–2 minutes until smooth and glossy.*

3 *Stir in chosen flavourings and beat until evenly blended.*

4 *Pour into prepared tin (pan), level the top and bake as required.*

CHOICE OF FLAVOURINGS

The following amounts are for a 2-egg quantity cake. Increase the suggested flavourings to suit the quantity being made.

Citrus – 10 ml/2 tsp/2 tsp finely grated orange, lemon or lime rind
Chocolate – add 15 ml/1 tbsp/1 tbsp cocoa blended with 15 ml/1 tbsp/1 tbsp boiling water, or 25 g/1 oz/scant ¼ cup chocolate dots, melted
Coffee – 10 ml/2 tsp/2 tsp coffee granules blended with 5 ml/1 tsp/1 tsp boiling water
Nuts – replace 25 g/1 oz/2 tbsp flour with finely ground nuts

Madeira Cake

A good, plain cake which can be made as an alternative to a light or rich fruit cake. It is firm and moist, can be flavoured to taste, and makes a good base for icing and decorating.

A madeira cake is traditionally used for decorative novelty cakes, as it provides a firm and lasting sponge base.

MADEIRA CAKE CHART

Cake Tin Sizes	15 cm/6 in Square	18 cm/7 in Square	20 cm/8 in Square	23 cm/9 in Square	25 cm/10 in Square	28 cm/11 in Square	30 cm/12 in Square
	18 cm/7 in Round	20 cm/8 in Round	23 cm/9 in Round	25 cm/10 in Round	28 cm/11 in Round	30 cm/12 in Round	33 cm/13 in Round
INGREDIENTS							
Plain (all-purpose) flour	225 g/ 8 oz/ 2 cups	350 g/ 12 oz/ 3 cups	450 g/ 1 lb/ 4 cups	500 g/ 1 lb 2 oz/ 4½ cups	575 g/ 1¼ lb/ 5 cups	675 g/ 1½ lb/ 6 cups	900 g/ 2 lb/ 8 cups
Baking powder	5 ml/ 1 tsp/ 1 tsp	7.5 ml/ 1½ tsp/ 1½ tsp	10 ml/ 2 tsp/ 2 tsp	12.5 ml/ 2½ tsp/ 2½ tsp	15 ml/ 3 tsp/ 3 tsp	17.5 ml/ 3½ tsp/ 3½ tsp	20 ml/ 4 tsp/ 4 tsp
Caster (superfine) sugar	175 g/ 6 oz/ ¾ cup	275 g/ 10 oz/ 1¼ cups	400 g/ 14 oz/ 1¾ cups	450 g/ 1 lb/ 2 cups	500 g/ 1 lb 2 oz/ 2¼ cups	625 g/ 1 lb 6 oz/ 2¾ cups	725 g/ 1 lb 10 oz/ 3¼ cups
Soft margarine	175 g/ 6 oz/ ¾ cup	275 g/ 10 oz/ 1¼ cups	400 g/ 14 oz/ 1¾ cups	450 g/ 1 lb/ 2 cups	500 g/ 1 lb 2 oz/ 2¼ cups	625 g/ 1 lb 6 oz/ 2¾ cups	725 g/ 1 lb 10 oz/ 3¼ cups
Size 3 eggs	3	5	7	8	10	12	13
Milk	30 ml/ 2 tbsp/ 2 tbsp	45 ml/ 3 tbsp/ 3 tbsp	55 ml/ 3½ tbsp/ 3½ tbsp	60 ml/ 4 tbsp/ 4 tbsp	70 ml/ 4½ tbsp/ 4½ tbsp	75 ml/ 5 tbsp/ 5 tbsp	85 ml/ 5½ tbsp/ 5½ tbsp
Approx. Cooking Time	1¼–1½ hours	1½–1¾ hours	1¾–2 hours	1¾–2 hours	2–2¼ hours	2¼–2½ hours	2½–2¾ hours

1 *Preheat the oven to 170°C/325°F/Gas 3.
Grease and line a deep cake tin (pan)
(see Lining Cake Tins [Pans]).*

2 *Sift flour and baking powder into a
mixing bowl. Add sugar, margarine,
eggs and milk. Mix together with a wooden
spoon, then beat for 1–2 minutes until
smooth and glossy. Alternatively, use an
electric mixer and beat for 1 minute only.*

3 *Add any flavourings desired and mix
until well blended.*

The following amounts are for a
3-egg quantity cake. Increase the
suggested flavourings to suit the
quantities being made.
Cherry – 175 g/6 oz/1 scant cup
glacé cherries, halved
Citrus – replace milk with lemon,
orange or lime juice and 5 ml/1 tsp/1
tsp of grated lemon, orange or lime
rind
Coconut – 50 g/2 oz/1 cup desiccated
(shredded) coconut
Nuts – replace 125 g/4 oz/1 cup flour
with ground almonds, hazelnuts,
walnuts or pecan nuts

4 *Place the mixture into the prepared tin
(pan) and spread evenly. Give the tin
(pan) a sharp tap to remove any air pockets.
Make a depression in the centre of the
mixture to ensure a level surface.*

5 *Bake the cake in the centre of the oven.
Follow the chart cooking times,
according to the size of the cake. It is cooked
when the cake springs back when lightly
pressed in the centre.*

STORING

Leave the cake to cool in the tin
(pan), then remove and cool
completely on a wire rack. Wrap in
plastic wrap or foil and store in a
cool place until required.

Rich Fruit Cake

This recipe makes a very moist rich cake suitable for any celebration. The cake can be made in stages, especially if time is short or if you are making more than one. It is easiest if the fruit is prepared and soaked overnight and the cake made the following day. Once the mixture is in the tin (pan), the surface may be covered with cling film (plastic wrap) and the cake stored in a cool place overnight if cooking is not possible on the day. The quantities have been carefully worked out so that the depth of each cake is the same. This is important when making several tiers for a wedding cake.

A classic rich fruit cake is traditionally used for christening cakes, as in the base for this delightful creation for a baby girl.

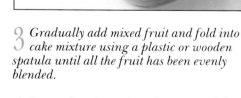

1 Into a large mixing bowl place the raisins, sultanas (golden raisins), currants, glacé cherries, mixed (candied) peel, flaked almonds, lemon rind and juice, brandy or sherry. Mix all the ingredients together until well blended, then cover the bowl with cling film (plastic wrap). Leave for several hours or overnight if required.

2 Pre-heat the oven to 140°C/275°F/Gas 1 and prepare a deep cake tin (see Lining Cake Tins [Pans]). Sift the flour and mixed spice into another mixing bowl. Add the ground almonds, sugar, butter, treacle (or molasses) and eggs. Mix together with a wooden spoon, then beat for 1–2 minutes until smooth and glossy. Alternatively, beat for 1 minute using an electric mixer.

3 Gradually add mixed fruit and fold into cake mixture using a plastic or wooden spatula until all the fruit has been evenly blended.

4 Spoon the mixture into the prepared tin (pan) and spread evenly. Give the container a few sharp bangs to level the mixture and to remove any air pockets. Smooth the surface with the back of a metal spoon, making a slight depression in the centre. The cake surface may be covered with cling film (plastic wrap) and left overnight in a cool place if required.

5 Bake the cake in the centre of the oven following the chart cooking time as a guide. Test the cake to see if it is cooked 30 minutes before the end of the cooking time. The cake should feel firm and, when a fine skewer is inserted into the centre, it should come out quite clean. If the cake is not cooked, retest it at 15-minute intervals. Remove the cake from the oven and allow it to cool in the tin (pan).

6 Turn the cake out of the tin (pan) but do not remove the lining paper as it helps to keep the moisture in. Spoon half quantity of brandy or sherry used in each cake over the top of the cooked cake and wrap in a double thickness of foil.

Store the cake in a cool, dry place on its base with the top uppermost for a week. Unwrap the cake and spoon over the remaining brandy or sherry. Rewrap well and invert the cake. Store it upside down, so the brandy or sherry moistens the top and helps to keep it flat.

The cake will store well for up to 3 months. If it is going to be stored for this length of time, add the brandy or sherry a little at a time at monthly intervals.

RICH FRUIT CAKE CHART

Cake Tin Sizes	12 cm/5 in Square	15 cm/6 in Square	18 cm/7 in Square	20 cm/8 in Square	23 cm/9 in Square	25 cm/10 in Square	28 cm/11 in Square	30 cm/12 in Square
	15 cm/6 in Round	18 cm/7 in Round	20 cm/8 in Round	23 cm/9 in Round	25 cm/10 in Round	28 cm/11 in Round	30 cm/12 in Round	33 cm/13 in Round
INGREDIENTS								
Raisins	200 g/ 7 oz/ 1⅓ cups	250 g/ 9 oz/ 1¾ cups	325 g/ 11 oz/ 2 cups	375 g/ 13 oz/ 2½ cups	425 g/ 15 oz/ 2⅔ cups	575 g/ 1¼ lb/ 3¾ cups	675 g/ 1½ lb/ 4½ cups	800 g/ 1¾ lb/ 5¼ cups
Sultanas (golden raisins)	125 g/ 4 oz/ ¾ cup	175 g/ 6 oz/ 1¼ cups	225 g/ 8 oz/ 1½ cups	275 g/ 10 oz/ 1⅔ cups	350 g/ 12 oz/ 2¼ cups	475 g/ 1 lb 1 oz/ 3¼ cups	600 g/ 1 lb 5 oz/ 4 cups	675 g/ 1½ lb/ 4½ cups
Currants	75 g/ 3 oz/ ⅔ cup	125 g/ 4 oz/ ¾ cup	175 g/ 6 oz/ 1¼ cups	225 g/ 8 oz/ 1⅔ cups	275 g/ 10 oz/ 2 cups	400 g/ 14 oz/ 3 cups	475 g/ 1 lb 1 oz/ 3½ cups	575 g/ 1¼ lb/ 4 cups
Glacé cherries, halved	75 g/ 3 oz/ ½ cup	75 g/ 3 oz/ ½ cup	150 g/ 5 oz/ 1 cup	175 g/ 6 oz/ 1 cup	200 g/ 7 oz/ 1⅓ cups	225 g/ 8 oz/ 1½ cups	275 g/ 10 oz/ 1⅔ cups	350 g/ 12 oz/ 2¼ cups
Mixed peel	25 g/ 1 oz/ ¼ cup	40 g/ 1½ oz/ ⅓ cup	50 g/ 2 oz/ ⅓ cup	75 g/ 3 oz/ ½ cup	125 g/ 4 oz/ ¾ cup	175 g/ 6 oz/ 1 cup	225 g/ 8 oz/ 1½ cups	275 g/ 10 oz/ 1⅔ cups
Flaked almonds	25 g/ 1 oz/ ¼ cup	40 g/ 1½ oz/ ⅓ cup	50 g/ 2 oz/ ½ cup	75 g/ 3 oz/ ¾ cup	125 g/ 4 oz/ 1 cup	175 g/ 6 oz/ 1⅔ cup	225 g/ 8 oz/ 2¼ cups	275 g/ 10 oz/ 2¾ cups
Lemon rind, coarsely grated	5 ml/ 1 tsp/ 1 tsp	7.5 ml/ 1½ tsp/ 1½ tsp	10 ml/ 2 tsp/ 2 tsp	12 ml/ 2½ tsp/ 2½ tsp	15 ml/ ½ fl oz/ 1 tbsp	25 ml/ 1½ tbsp/ 1½ tbsp	25 ml/ 1½ tbsp/ 1½ tbsp	30 ml/ 2 tbsp/ 2 tbsp
Lemon juice	15 ml/ 1 tbsp/ 1 tbsp	25 ml/ 1½ tbsp/ 1½ tbsp	30 ml/ 2 tbsp/ 2 tbsp	40 ml/ 2½ tbsp/ 2½ tbsp	45 ml/ 3 tbsp/ 3 tbsp	60 ml/ 4 tbsp/ 4 tbsp	75 ml/ 5 tbsp/ 5 tbsp	90 ml/ 6 tbsp/ 6 tbsp
Brandy or sherry	15 ml/ 1 tbsp/ 1 tbsp	30 ml/ 2 tbsp/ 2 tbsp	45 ml/ 3 tbsp/ 3 tbsp	60 ml/ 4 tbsp/ 4 tbsp	75 ml/ 5 tbsp/ 5 tbsp	90 ml/ 6 tbsp/ 6 tbsp	105 ml/ 7 tbsp/ 7 tbsp	120 ml/ 8 tbsp/ ½ cup
Plain (all-purpose) flour	175 g/ 6 oz/ 1½ cups	200 g/ 7 oz/ 1¾ cups	250 g/ 9 oz/ 2¼ cups	325 g/ 11 oz/ 2¾ cups	400 g/ 14 oz/ 3½ cups	500 g/ 1 lb 2 oz/ 4½ cups	625 g/ 1 lb 6 oz/ 5½ cups	725 g/ 1 lb 10 oz/ 6½ cups
Ground mixed spice	5 ml/ 1 tsp/ 1 tsp	7.5 ml/ 1½ tsp/ 1½ tsp	12 ml/ 2½ tsp/ 2½ tsp	15 ml/ 1 tbsp/ 1 tbsp	18 ml/ 1¼ tbsp/ 1¼ tbsp	25 ml/ 1½ tbsp/ 1½ tbsp	30 ml/ 2 tbsp/ 2 tbsp	70 ml/ 3½ tbsp/ 3½ tbsp
Ground almonds	25 g/ 1 oz/ ¼ cup	40 g/ 1½ oz/ ⅓ cup	65 g/ 2½ oz/ ⅔ cup	125 g/ 4 oz/ 1¼ cups	150 g/ 5 oz/ 1⅓ cups	225 g/ 8 oz/ 2¼ cups	275 g/ 10 oz/ 2¾ cups	350 g/ 12 oz/ 3⅓ cups
Dark brown sugar	125 g/ 4 oz/ ¾ cup	150 g/ 5 oz/ 1 cup	200 g/ 7 oz/ 1⅓ cups	250 g/ 9 oz/ 1⅔ cups	350 g/ 12 oz/ 2¼ cups	475 g/ 1 lb 1 oz/ 3⅓ cups	575 g/ 1¼ lb/ 3¾ cups	650 g/ 1 lb 7 oz/ 4½ cups
Butter, softened	125 g/ 4 oz/ ½ cup	150 g/ 5 oz/ ⅔ cup	200 g/ 7 oz/ 1 cup	250 g/ 9 oz/ 1¼ cups	350 g/ 12 oz/ 1½ cups	475 g/ 1 lb 1 oz/ 2¼ cups	575 g/ 1¼ lb/ 2½ cups	650 g/ 1 lb 7 oz/ 3 cups
Black treacle (or molasses)	10 ml/ ½ tbsp/ ½ tbsp	15 ml/ 1 tbsp/ 1 tbsp	25 ml/ 1½ tbsp/ 1½ tbsp	30 ml/ 2 tbsp/ 2 tbsp	40 ml/ 2½ tbsp/ 2½ tbsp	45 ml/ 3 tbsp/ 3 tbsp	55 ml/ 3½ tbsp/ 3½ tbsp	60 ml/ 4 tbsp/ 4 tbsp
Eggs	2	3	4	5	6	7	8	10
Approx. Cooking Time	2¼–2½ hours	2½–2¾ hours	3–3½ hours	3¼–3¾ hours	3¾–4¼ hours	4–4½ hours	4½–5¼ hours	5¼–5¾ hours

Whisked Sponge Cake

This light sponge can be used for making Swiss rolls, cakes or gateaux.

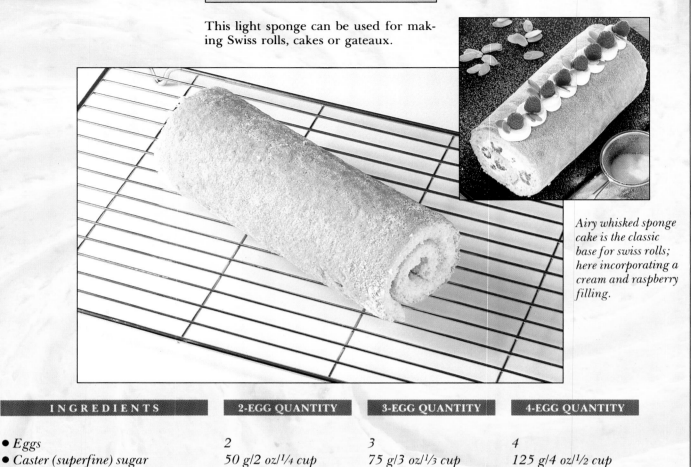

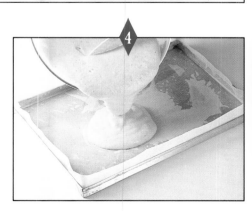

Airy whisked sponge cake is the classic base for swiss rolls; here incorporating a cream and raspberry filling.

INGREDIENTS	2-EGG QUANTITY	3-EGG QUANTITY	4-EGG QUANTITY
● Eggs	2	3	4
● Caster (superfine) sugar	50 g/2 oz/¼ cup	75 g/3 oz/⅓ cup	125 g/4 oz/½ cup
● Plain (all-purpose) flour	50 g/2 oz/½ cup	75 g/3 oz/¾ cup	125 g/4 oz/1 cup

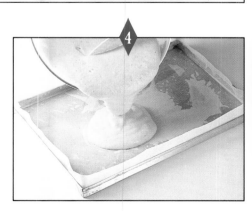

1 *Preheat the oven to 180°C/350°F/Gas 4. Prepare the tin (pan) according to the recipe.*

2 *Whisk together the eggs and sugar in a heatproof bowl until thoroughly blended. Place the bowl over a saucepan of simmering water and whisk until thick and pale. Remove the bowl from the saucepan and continue whisking until the mixture is cool and leaves a thick trail on the surface when the beaters are lifted.*

3 *Sift the flour onto the surface, add any desired flavourings and, using a plastic spatula, carefully fold the flour into the mixture until smooth.*

4 *Pour into a prepared tin (pan), tilt to level and bake as required.*

Butter Icing

This most popular and well-known icing is made quickly with butter and icing (confectioners) sugar. Add your choice of flavourings and colourings to vary the cake.

INGREDIENTS

Makes 450 g/1 lb/1 lb
- *125 g/4 oz/1/2 cup unsalted butter, softened*
- *225 g/8 oz/2 cups icing (confectioners) sugar, sifted*
- *10 ml/2 tsp/2 tsp milk*
- *5 ml/1 tsp/1 tsp vanilla essence (extract)*

Butter icing is a quick and attractive topping for a cake.

1 Place the butter in a bowl. Using a wooden spoon or an electric mixer, beat until light and fluffy.

2 Stir in the icing (confectioners) sugar, milk and vanilla essence (extract), and/ or flavourings until evenly mixed, then beat well until light and smooth.

3 Spread the icing over the cake with a metal palette knife (spatula).

CHOICE OF FLAVOURINGS

Citrus – replace milk and vanilla essence (extract) with orange, lemon or lime juice and 10 ml/2 tsp/2 tsp finely grated orange, lemon or lime rind. Omit the rind if the icing is to be piped.

Chocolate – 15 ml/1 tbsp/1 tbsp cocoa powder blended with 15 ml/1 tbsp/1 tbsp boiling water, cooled
Coffee – 10 ml/2 tsp/2 tsp coffee granules blended with 15 ml/1 tbsp/1 tbsp boiling water, cooled

Chocolate Fudge Icing

A rich glossy icing which sets like chocolate fudge, it is versatile enough to smoothly coat, swirl or pipe, depending on the temperature of the icing when it is used.

INGREDIENTS

Makes 450 g/1 lb/1 lb
- *125 g/4 oz/4 squares plain (semisweet) chocolate*
- *50 g/2 oz/¼ cup unsalted butter*
- *1 egg, beaten*
- *175 g/6 oz/1 cup icing (confectioners) sugar, sifted*

Chocolate fudge icing is smooth and sumptuous, with a rich dark colour that contrasts beautifully with fresh flowers in a simple but effective decoration.

1 *Place the chocolate and butter in a heatproof bowl over a saucepan of hot water.*

2 *Stir occasionally with a wooden spoon until melted. Add the egg and beat until smooth.*

3 *Remove the bowl from the saucepan and stir in the icing (confectioners) sugar, then beat until smooth and glossy.*

4 *Pour immediately over the cake for a smooth finish, or leave to cool for a thicker spreading or piping consistency as here.*

American Frosting

A light marshmallow icing which crisps on the outside when left to dry, this versatile frosting may be swirled or peaked into a soft coating.

Makes 350 g/12 oz/³⁄₄ lb
- 1 egg white
- 30 ml/2 tbsp/2 tbsp water
- 15 ml/1 tbsp/1 tbsp golden syrup (light corn syrup)
- 5 ml/1 tsp/1 tsp cream of tartar
- 175 g/6 oz/1 cup icing (confectioners) sugar, sifted

American frosting makes a light, fluffy yet crisp topping, its soft white contrasting well with chocolate caraque.

1 Place the egg white, water, golden syrup (light corn syrup) and cream of tartar in a heatproof bowl. Whisk together until thoroughly blended.

2 Stir the icing (confectioners) sugar into the mixture and place the bowl over a saucepan of simmering water. Whisk until the mixture becomes thick and white.

3 Remove the bowl from the saucepan and continue to whisk the frosting until cool and thick, and the mixture stands up in soft peaks.

4 Use immediately to fill or cover cakes.

Homemade Marzipan

INGREDIENTS

Makes 450 g/1 lb/1 lb
- 225 g/8 oz/2¼ cups ground almonds
- 125 g/4 oz/½ cup caster (superfine) sugar
- 125 g/4 oz/¾ cup icing (confectioners) sugar, sieved (sifted)
- 5 ml/1 tsp/1 tsp lemon juice
- few drops almond flavouring
- 1 (size 4) egg, or 1 (size 2) egg white

Marzipan is extremely versatile; here it has been used in place of icing for this unusual Christmas cake.

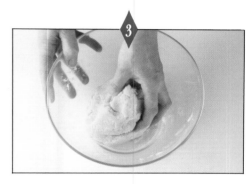

1 *Place the ground almonds, caster (superfine) and icing (confectioners) sugars into a bowl. Stir until evenly mixed.*

2 *Make a 'well' in the centre and add the lemon juice, almond flavouring and enough egg or egg white to mix to a soft but firm dough, using a wooden spoon.*

3 *Form the marzipan into a ball. Lightly dust a surface with icing (confectioners) sugar and knead the marzipan until smooth and free from cracks.*

4 *Wrap in cling film (plastic wrap) or store in a polythene (polyethylene) bag until ready for use. Tint with food colouring if required, and use for moulding shapes or covering cakes.*

MARZIPAN CHART

Cake Tin Sizes	12 cm/5 in Square	15 cm/6 in Square	18 cm/7 in Square	20 cm/8 in Square	23 cm/9 in Square	25 cm/10 in Square	28 cm/11 in Square	30 cm/12 in Square
	15 cm/6 in Round	18 cm/7 in Round	20 cm/8 in Round	23 cm/9 in Round	25 cm/10 in Round	28 cm/11 in Round	30 cm/12 in Round	33 cm/13 in Round
QUANTITIES								
Apricot glaze	25 ml/ 1½ tbsp/ 1½ tbsp	30 ml/ 2 tbsp/ 2 tbsp	40 ml/ 2½ tbsp/ 2½ tbsp	45 ml/ 3 tbsp/ 3 tbsp	55 ml/ 3½ tbsp/ 3½ tbsp	60 ml/ 4 tbsp/ 4 tbsp	75 ml/ 4½ tbsp/ 4½ tbsp	75 ml/ 5 tbsp/ 5 tbsp
Marzipan	450 g/ 1 lb/ 1 lb	675 g/ 1½ lb/ 1½ lb	800 g/ 1¾ lb/ 1¾ lb	900 g/ 2 lb/ 2 lb	1.1 kg/ 2½ lb/ 2½ lb	1.5 kg/ 3¼ lb/ 3¼ lb	1.8 kg/ 4 lb/ 4 lb	1.9 kg/ 4¼ lb/ 4¼ lb

Royal Icing

This icing made with fresh egg whites is traditionally used to cover celebration cakes. Depending upon its consistency, it may be used for flat icing, peaked icing or piping designs on to cakes.

INGREDIENTS

Makes 450 g/1 lb/1½ cups
- *2 egg whites*
- *1.5 ml/¼ tsp/¼ tsp lemon juice*
- *450 g/1 lb/3 cups icing (confectioners) sugar, sieved (sifted)*
- *5 ml/1 tsp/1 tsp glycerine*

Peaked royal icing has been used to coat little fruit cakes for a witty and attractive festive gift.

Royal Icing Consistencies

The consistency of royal icing varies for different uses. Stiff icing is necessary for piping, slightly softer for flat icing or peaked icing, and slacker for run-outs.

PIPING CONSISTENCY
When a wooden spoon is drawn out of the icing, it should form a fine, sharp point, termed as 'sharp peak'. This consistency flows easily for piping but retains a definite shape produced by the nozzle.

FLAT OR PEAKED ICING CONSISTENCY
When the spoon is drawn out of the icing it should form a fine point which curves over at the end, termed as 'soft peak'. This consistency spreads smoothly and creates a flat finish, but also pulls up into sharp or soft peaks.

RUN-OUTS
Use soft peak consistency to pipe the outlines, and thick cream consistency to fill in the shapes. This consistency flows to fill in the run-outs, but holds a rounded shape within the piped lines.

1 *Place the egg whites and lemon juice in a clean bowl. Using a clean wooden spoon, stir to break up the egg whites. Add sufficient icing (confectioners) sugar and mix well to form the consistency of unwhipped cream.*

2 *Continue mixing and adding small quantities of sugar every few minutes, until the desired consistency has been reached. Mix well after each addition of sugar.*

3 *Stir in the glycerine until the icing is well blended.*

How to Marzipan a Cake for Sugarpaste (Fondant Icing)

APRICOT GLAZE

It is always a good idea to make a large quantity of apricot glaze, especially when making celebration cakes. Use for brushing the cakes before applying the marzipan, or for glazing fruits on gateaux and cakes.

INGREDIENTS

Makes 450 g/1 lb/1 lb
- *450 g/1 lb/1½ cups apricot jam*
- *45 ml/3 tbsp/3 tbsp water*

1 *Place jam and water into a saucepan, heat gently, stirring occasionally until melted. Boil rapidly for 1 minute, then strain through a sieve (strainer).*

2 *Rub through as much fruit as possible, using a wooden spoon. Discard the skins left in the sieve (strainer).*

STORING

Pour the glaze into a clean, hot jar, seal with a clean lid and cool. Refrigerate for up to 2 months.

1 *Unwrap the cake and remove the lining paper. Place the cake on a cakeboard and roll the top with a rolling pin to flatten slightly.*

2 *Brush the top and sides of the cake with apricot glaze (see above), and dust the surface lightly with sieved (sifted) icing (confectioners) sugar.*

3 *Knead the marzipan into a smooth ball. Roll out to a 5 mm/¼ in thickness, to match the shape of the cake, and large enough to cover the top and sides, about 5–7.5 cm/2–3 in larger. Make sure the marzipan moves freely, then roll the marzipan loosely around the rolling pin.*

4 *Place the supported marzipan over the cake and carefully unroll so that the marzipan falls evenly over the cake. Working from the centre of the cake, carefully smooth the marzipan over the top and down the sides, lifting the edges slightly to allow the marzipan to fit at the base of the cake without stretching or tearing the top edge.*

5 *Using a sharp knife, trim the excess marzipan from the base of the cake, cutting down on to the board.*

6 *Using clean, dry hands, gently rub the top of the cake in circular movements to make a smooth glossy finish to the marzipan.*

7 *Leave in a warm, dry place for at least 2 hours before covering with sugarpaste (fondant).*

To Cover Any Shaped Cake with Sugarpaste (Fondant)

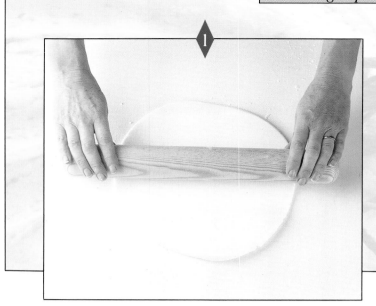

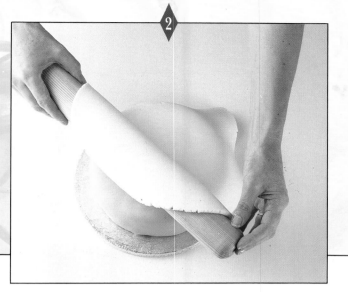

1 *Place the marzipanned cake, on the cakeboard, onto a turntable and brush the surface evenly with a little sherry or cooled boiled water. Dust a work surface with sieved (sifted) icing (confectioners) sugar to prevent the sugarpaste from sticking. Roll out the sugarpaste (fondant) to 5 mm/¼ in thickness, using more sieved (sifted) icing (confectioners) sugar if necessary, to the chosen shape of the cake.*

2 *Trim the sugarpaste (fondant) to 6.5 cm/2½ in larger than the top of the cake, making sure the icing moves freely. Lift the sugarpaste carefully over the top of the cake, supported by a rolling pin. Brush off any excess icing (confectioners) sugar. Unroll the sugarpaste over the cake to cover evenly.*

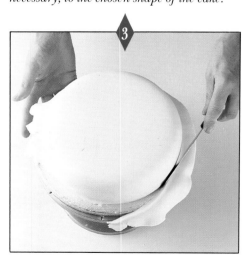

3 *Dust your hands with cornflour (cornstarch), and smooth the icing over the top and then down the sides of the cake. Ease the excess icing toward the base, excluding any air bubbles between the surfaces. Trim off excess icing at base of cake using a small knife.*

4 *Dust your hands with more cornflour (cornstarch), and gently rub the surface of the sugarpaste in circular movements to make it smooth and glossy. Place the cake in a cake box and leave in a warm, dry place to dry the sugarpaste.*

5 *Knead the trimmings together and seal in cling film (plastic wrap) or a polythene (polyethylene) bag and use to cover the cakeboard, or for decorations.*

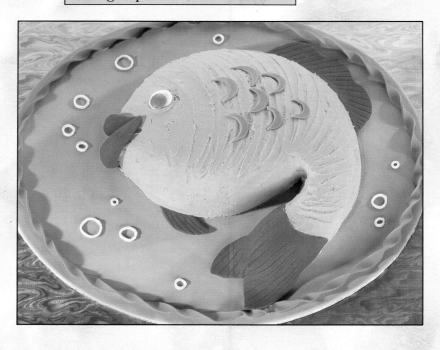

To Cover Any Shaped
Cakeboard with
Sugarpaste (Fondant)

*Complete the effect
of a novelty or
classic cake by
continuing the
coloured fondant or
sugarpaste covering
onto the cakeboard.*

1 *Lightly dust a surface with icing
(confectioners) sugar. Tint the
sugarpaste (fondant) to the required colour
to match the cake. Brush the cakeboard with
a little apricot glaze.*

2 *Roll out the sugarpaste (fondant) to 5
mm/¼ in thickness to the shape of the
cakeboard. Ensure the sugarpaste moves
freely and lift over the cakeboard. Dust your
hands with cornflour (cornstarch), and
smooth the surface, trimming off excess
icing using a small palette knife (spatula).
Keep the blade level with the edge of the
board and take care to keep the edge of the
sugarpaste (fondant) straight.*

3 *Leave the iced board in a warm place
overnight to dry. Then place the iced
cake carefully in position.*

FOOD COLOURINGS
AND TINTS

Food colourings and tints have changed dramatically over the last few years. At one time food colourings were only available in bottles in a range of primary colours. These liquid colours are still available from most supermarkets and shops and are adequate for tinting icings, frosting, butter icing, marzipan and sugarpaste. With careful blending many other colours and shades can be achieved. Since the colourings are fairly diluted, it is impossible to achieve a richer colour without diluting the consistency of the icing. So for stronger colours, concentrated food colouring pastes produce better results.

PASTE, POWDER AND LIQUID COLOURS

In specialist cake-icing and decorating shops, food colourings are available in a far greater range. Good quality colours appear as pastes, powders and liquids. They are very concentrated and need to be added drop by drop, using a cocktail stick to stir and carefully tint the icing to a delicate shade. An exceptional variety of colours are available so there is no need to blend the colours to obtain the shade of icing you want. Since they are so concentrated, the consistency of the icing is not affected. The colours are also permanent and do not fade.

Remember that food colourings, when added to icings or kneaded into marzipan or sugarpaste, change on standing and dry a deeper or a lighter colour than when first mixed. Colour sample amounts of icing in the daylight and leave them for at least 15 minutes to assess if you have achieved the desired colour. If you are matching icing with fabrics or flowers, allow coloured samples to dry thoroughly before deciding. If several batches of coloured icing are to be made, keep some icing in reserve so the colour can be matched. Always remember that a cake should look edible, so keep the colours to pastel shades – a hint of colour is better than too much.

Celebration cakes may require more subtle shading and tinting. Moulded and cut-out flowers, sugar pieces and cakes' surfaces can now be coloured with 'blossom tints', or painted with 'lustre colours' when the flowers, sugar pieces or icings

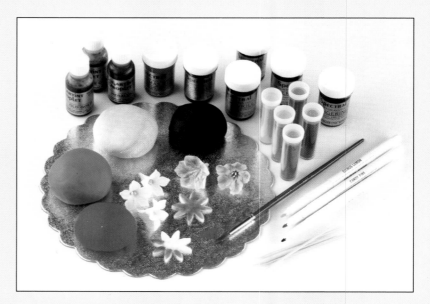

are dry. This also gives you an opportunity to add colour at the last minute, and prevents the risk of colours running into the icing when the atmosphere is damp. These products also hold their colour without fading. Such specialist food colours are available only from cake-decorating shops.

FOOD-COLOURING PENS

These pens look like fibre-tip pens but are filled with edible food colourings. They come in a range of primary colours as well as black, brown and purple. Their uses are endless, especially for quickly decorating, writing or applying details to models or sugar pieces.

Use them like a pen to write or draw a design onto dry royal icing run-outs, small sugar plaques or even to mark a design directly onto an iced cake. But these pens are indelible – so make no mistakes!

Marzipan or sugarpaste (fondant) is easily tinted with food colouring; break off small pieces and work in gradually until evenly blended.

Marbling

Sugarpaste (fondant) lends itself to tinting in all shades, and a very effective way of colouring is to marble the paste. Use it to cover a cake and the cakeboard completely and use the trimmings for cut-out or moulded decorations.

1 Add a few drops of food colouring in drops over the icing.

2 Do not knead the food colouring fully into the icing.

3 When it is rolled out, the colour is dispersed in such a way that it gives a marbled appearance to the sugarpaste (fondant).

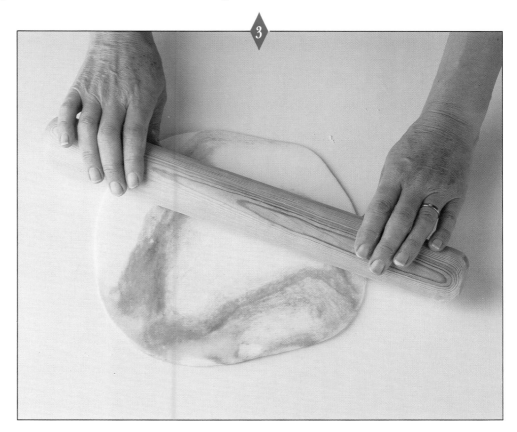

Marbling is a wonderful effect easily achieved with sugarpaste or fondant and edible food colourings, as shown with this blue and orange candle-shaped novelty cake.

USEFUL SUPPLIERS AND ADDRESSES

Great Britain

THE BRITISH SUGARCRAFT GUILD
Wellington House, Messeter Place, Eltham, London SE9 5DP.
CAKE ART LTD
Wholesale suppliers of icings and equipment. Unit 16, Crown Close, Crown Industrial Estate, Priors Wood, Taunton, Somerset TA2 8RX.
SUGARCRAFT SUPPLIERS PME (HARROW) LTD
Suppliers of decorating equipment. Brember Road, South Harrow, Middlesex HA2 8UN.
JF RENSHAW LTD
Suppliers of icings. Locks Lane, Mitcham, Surrey CR4 2XG.
ESSEX ICING CENTRE
Suppliers of materials and equipment. 20 Western Road, Billericay, Essex CM12 9DZ.
INVICTA BAKEWARE LTD
Manufacturers and suppliers of bakery equipment. Westgate Business Park, Westgate Carr Road, Pickering, North Yorkshire YO18 8LX.
CRANHAM CATERING
Suppliers of materials and equipment. 95 Front Lane, Cranham, Upminster, Essex RM14 1XN.
CRAIGMILLAR
Suppliers of icings. Stadium Road, Bromborough, Wirral, Merseyside LO2 3NU.
PROMODEM LTD
Technical consultancy and suppliers of cake tilters. 141 Grange Road, Great Burstead, Billericay, Essex CM11 2SA.
SQUIRES KITCHEN
Squire House, 3 Waverley Lane, Farnham, Surrey GU9 8BB.
E RUSSUM & SONS
Edward House, Tenter Street, Rotherham.
THE HOUSE OF SUGARCRAFT
Suppliers of flower cutters, powder and paste colours and piping tubes. Unit 10, Broxhead Industrial Estate, Lindford Road, Bordon, Hampshire GU35 0NY.
CEL CAKES
Suppliers of modelling tools, containers and display cabinets. Springfield House, Gate Helmsley, York, North Yorkshire YO4 1NF.
JENNY CAMPBELL TRADING/B R MATTHEWS AND SON
12 Gypsy Hill, Upper Norwood, London SE19 1NN.
CYNTHIA VENN
3 Anker Lane, Stubbington, Fareham, Hampshire PO14 3HF.
KNIGHTSBRIDGE BUSINESS CENTRE (WILTON UK)
Knightsbridge, Cheltenham, Gloucestershire GL51 9TA.
RAINBOW RIBBONS
Unit D5, Romford Seedbed Centre, Davidson Way, Romford, Essex RM7 0AZ.

North America

ICES (INTERNATIONAL CAKE EXPLORATION SOCIETY)
Membership enquiries: 3087–30th St. S.W., Ste.101, Grandville, MI 49418.
MAID OF SCANDINAVIA
Equipment, supplies, courses, magazine Mailbox News. *3244 Raleigh Avenue, Minneapolis, MN 55416.*
WILTON ENTERPRISES INC
2240 West 75th Street, Woodridge, Illinois 60517.
HOME CAKE ARTISTRY INC
1002 North Central, Suite 511, Richardson, Texas 75080.
LORRAINE'S INC
148 Broadway, Hanover, MA 02339.
CREATIVE TOOLS LTD
3 Tannery Court, Richmond Hill, Ontario, Canada L4C 7V5.
MCCALL'S SCHOOL OF CAKE DECORATING INC
3810 Bloor Street, Islington, Ontario, Canada M9B 6C2.

Australia

AUSTRALIAN NATIONAL CAKE DECORATORS' ASSOCIATION
PO Box 321, Plympton, SA 5038.
CAKE DECORATING ASSOCIATION OF VICTORIA
President, Shirley Vaas, 4 Northcote Road, Ocean Grove, Victoria 3226.
CAKE DECORATING GUILD OF NEW SOUTH WALES
President, Fay Gardiner, 4 Horsley Cres, Melba, Act, 2615.
CAKE DECORATING ASSOCIATION OF TASMANIA
Secretary, Jenny Davis, 29 Honolulu Street, Midway Point, Tasmania 7171.
CAKE DECORATORS' ASSOCIATION OF SOUTH AUSTRALIA
Secretary, Lorraine Joliffe, Pindari, 12 Sussex Crescent, Morphet Vale, SA 5162.
CAKE ORNAMENT CO
156 Alfred Street, Fortitude Valley, Brisbane 4006.

INDEX

ACKNOWLEDGEMENTS

Janice Murfitt would like to thank the following: Mavis Giles for her unfailing ability to type illegible copy at a minute's notice; Jean Ainger for supplying equipment and sugarcraft props for photography; Cake Fayre, 11 Saddlers Walk, 44 East Street, Chichester, W Sussex, PO19 1HQ (Tel. 0243 771857).

Louise Pickford and Sarah Maxwell would like to thank Teresa Goldfinch for her assistance with home economy.